Multiple Intelligences
made easy

Multiple Intelligences
made easy

Strategies for
Your Curriculum

Bonita DeAmicis

Zephyr Press

Tucson, Arizona

About Zephyr Press

Founded in 1979 in Tucson, Arizona, Zephyr Press continually strives to provide quality, innovative products for our customers, with the goal of improving learning opportunities for all children. With a focus on gifted education, multiple intelligences, and brain-compatible learning, Zephyr Press material is selected to help *all* children reach their highest potential.

Multiple Intelligences Made Easy
Strategies for Your Curriculum

Grades 3–6

©1999 by Bonita DeAmicis
Printed in the United States of America

ISBN 1-56976-101-9

Editors: Jennifer Wedel and Stacey Shropshire
Cover design: Stirling Crebbs
Design and production: Daniel Miedaner

Published by:
Zephyr Press
P.O. Box 66006
Tucson, AZ 85728-6006
800-232-2187
www.zephyrpress.com
www.i-home-school.com

 Zephyr Press is a registered trademark of Zephyr Press, Inc.

Library of Congress Cataloging-in-Publication Data

DeAmicis, Bonita, 1961-
    Multiple intelligences made easy : strategies for your curriculum / Bonita
DeAmicis
        p.   cm.
    Includes bibliographical references (p.).
    ISBN 1-56976-101-9
    1. Learning. 2. Cognitive styles. 3. Curriculum planning.
4. Teaching.   I. Title.
LB1060.D42   1997
370.15'23—dc20   96-30400

In loving memory of
Edith Hunt

1908–1986

Acknowledgments

I wish to express gratitude to the many people who offered input, encouragement, and support to make this book a reality. Thank you first to my husband, Joe, and daughters, Carmel and Juliet, for giving me the strong foundation of love and home; without you this project would never have happened. Thank you to my sister, Debbie Treiber, for being an inspiration, for all the feedback and input, and for encouraging me not to discount my thoughts and ideas. Thank you to the rest of my family for all the words of encouragement. Thank you to the principals and teachers of Emblem and Bouquet Canyon Elementary Schools, Saugus Union School District, for inviting me to teach in their GATE programs and supporting my efforts in creating these lessons; special thanks to Tiffany Branda for your special interest in this project. Thank you also to my friends Kristi Hann and Nancy Broschart for the countless hours of baby-sitting, not to mention the additional editing duties. Thank you to Keith Rogers for sharing with me the news about the naturalist intelligence. Special thanks to Joey Tanner, the publisher of Zephyr Press, for giving me the opportunity to publish my ideas, as well as to Stacy Tanner, who showed considerable humor, patience, and support in the contract process, and to Jennifer Wedel, an excellent editor, and all the other people at Zephyr Press who put in the hours to bring this book to fruition. Last but not least, I wish to thank Howard Gardner and the many researchers, teachers, and writers who provided the framework for me to learn about multiple intelligence theory; wherever I do the theory justice, you deserve the credit. Wherever I might misuse, misinterpret, or befuddle, the responsibility lies with me.

Contents

Introduction

About This Book

When you first learned about multiple intelligence theory (MI), did your creative self shout, "Drop everything! Redesign your class framework and embark on this new and exciting venture!"? Did your practical mind groan and remind you that you were already overwhelmed and had no room for more on your to-do list?

You are far from alone. Many teachers tell me they browse through and even purchase MI books, but can never seem to follow through and introduce the theory into their classrooms. Why? Because they don't have their students' best interests at heart? Of course not. More likely, the reluctance stems from the fact that implementing most MI curriculum plans requires a daunting amount of time and money: planning time, personal learning time, and classroom time, and the purchase of endless special supplies and materials.

If this scenario sounds familiar, you have come to the right place. With the help of the strategies in this book, you can stop *planning* and start *doing*—tomorrow! With minimal research or planning, and using standard classroom materials, you can use my step-by-step instructions to introduce your students and yourself to MI without having to reconstruct your entire classroom or curriculum.

This book is a place to get your feet wet, to learn inexpensive and easy ways to bring multiple intelligence experiences into your classroom and your *existing curriculum,* and to develop a personal menu of MI favorites. Use this book as a walker to get yourself started; once the central concepts of MI become familiar to you and to your students, you will find it much easier and more attractive to continue with more complex, holistic MI teaching strategies. The bibliography lists a number of excellent resources to initiate a deeper level of MI use in the classroom.

If you are already deeply immersed in the multiple intelligence approach to education, this book is the perfect desktop resource, a quick and easy way to find and include one or two new multiple intelligence strategies in your lesson plans each week.

A Multiple Intelligences Primer

Multiple intelligence theory was developed by Howard Gardner of Harvard University's Project Zero. In 1981, he received a MacArthur Prize Fellowship recognizing the importance of his research into the nature of human intelligence, which continues to this day. In reviewing the results of research studies into the biological and cultural bases of intelligence, Gardner found information that contradicted the traditional and limiting definition of intelligence as the measurement provided by an IQ test. Gardner proposed that humans have various intelligences that involve different parts of the brain but that are interrelated and work together in an integrated manner when we learn or think. Each intelligence has an impact on the others, and strengthening one can help develop the others. People generally have all intelligences but often are more genetically predisposed to using or developed in one area than another. When Gardner first introduced the theory of multiple intelligence he used strict criteria to identify seven intelligences. He has since added an eighth intelligence, the naturalist.

MI theory challenges many modern assumptions about what constitutes intelligence and creativity and questions conventional educational approaches that disregard the specific needs and development of the individual learner. Most important for educators, the multiple intelligences are teachable and *can be developed*.

Traditional teaching—in elementary through university education—focuses on two of the intelligences: verbal-linguistic and mathematical-logical. However, not all students have well-developed verbal or mathematical abilities. Integration of more intelligences into the curriculum can greatly enhance student understanding and learning. When students who are weak in verbal and logical intelligences approach a subject from one of their stronger intelligences, not only can they learn faster and retain more, but they can also strengthen the areas of intelligence that were weak to begin with. Students who are strong in verbal-linguistic and mathematical-logical intelligences also benefit from an application of more intelligences because their brains are not limited to using those two capacities. Every individual has her own intelligence blueprint, and that blueprint changes as we grow and develop. Using multiple intelligence approaches ensures balanced development.

What Is Intelligence?

According to Gardner (1983), "An intelligence entails the ability to solve problems or fashion products that are of consequence in a particular cultural setting or community." Gardner developed a specific set of criteria to verify that an intelligence exists. An intelligence must be based in biology, as revealed through research into the breakdown of skills in people who sustain brain injuries, as well as in the study of special populations (autistic savants, prodigies, and so on). An intelligence must have core operations that respond to outside stimulation (such as sensitivity to pitch in the musical intelligence). An intelligence should lend itself to being captured in a symbol system (for example, in the musical intelligence, the symbol system is musical notation). And, finally, an intelligence should be a valued capacity across various cultures (Gardner 1983).

The Original Seven Intelligences

Verbal-Linguistic

This intelligence is word-think. People strong in this intelligence like words. They like talking, reading, writing, and thinking with words. They like to express themselves through spoken and written language. They are public speakers, poets, persuasive writers, speech writers, and humorists. A child who likes to play with words (tongue twisters and puns), a child who can successfully debate and discuss an issue, a child who loves to write and read is demonstrating development of this intelligence.

Teaching via verbal intelligence already happens daily in the traditional classroom, maybe because it relates to the basic skills of reading and writing or because teachers tend to be strong in this intelligence.

Mathematical-Logical

The mathematical-logical intelligence is the arithmetic part of the 3 Rs equation: number-think. People strong in this intelligence like logical, systematic, sequenced ideas. They enjoy patterns, abstract symbols, math, problem-solving, and puzzles. They are scientists, mathematicians, strategic planners, accountants, and financial analysts. A child who loves math or science, a child who enjoys any kind of puzzle or detective story in which an unknown is methodically resolved, a child who likes to outline or list ideas, or a child who likes to write in code is demonstrating strength in this intelligence.

The mathematical-logical intelligence is one of the most commonly taught intelligences in schools today, partially because the intelligence is crucial to keeping our students at the forefront of our increasingly computerized and technological world. Its predominance may also be due to the fact that people attracted to the teaching profession are often well-developed in the mathematical-logical intelligence.

Visual-Spatial

This intelligence involves picture- and space-think. People strong in this intelligence like pictures, colors, shapes, and the space around them. They like to use their imaginations, to daydream, and to visualize the future or a story they are reading. They are good at finding their way around new places. They can design space and ways to use it. They are artists, decorators, photographers, architects, filmmakers, and map makers. A child who loves looking at art, drawing, sculpting, and model making, who loves to explore new places and can quickly find his or her way around, who likes to make jigsaw puzzles, or who likes to daydream a story he or she is reading is demonstrating a strength in this intelligence.

Bodily-Kinesthetic

This intelligence is body-think. People strong in this intelligence have good coordination and a high awareness of their own bodies, and are physically expressive. They like to play sports, dance, act, and make things. They are our athletes and coaches, choreographers and dancers, inventors, and sculptors. A child who loves sports, dance, acting, and exercise, who can quickly imitate a physical movement, or who likes to demonstrate how something works is strong in this intelligence.

Musical-Rhythmic

This intelligence incorporates sound-think. People strong in this intelligence are sensitive to the sounds and rhythmic patterns around them. They like music, speech patterns and accents, learning and singing songs, and tapping out beats. They are musicians, singers, dancers, sound-effects engineers, and composers. A child who loves listening to music or playing an instrument, a child who loves to sing, or a child who enjoys mimicking sounds and rhythms is demonstrating a strength in this intelligence.

Interpersonal

This intelligence incorporates group-think. People strong in this intelligence love to work in teams and meet new people. They like to talk to a partner, solve a problem by talking through it, react and respond to someone else's ideas, and listen sensitively to the feelings of others. They are team players, managers, psychologists, mediators, and diplomats. A child who loves to interact, a child who likes to guess what others are thinking and feeling, or a child who likes to work cooperatively on a team is demonstrating strength in this intelligence.

Intrapersonal

This intelligence reflects self-think. People strong in this intelligence love to work alone and ponder the inner workings of their own brains. They are in tune with their thoughts and feelings and therefore can be attuned to and intuitive about others. They have strong opinions and beliefs, are strong willed and self-confident about their ideas. They are philosophers, diary writers, and essayists. A child who likes to work alone, to sit and ponder ideas, a child who is clear and expressive about her own thoughts and feelings, or a child who sometimes surprises us with insight or wisdom is demonstrating a strength in this intelligence.

And Many More?

Gardner stresses that it is the pluralistic nature of intelligence that needs our attention as educators. Whether intelligences that meet the established criteria add up to seven, eight, or twenty-nine is less important than that we recognize that humans hold varied and vast intelligence. Any and all intelligence capacities exist in various degrees in each person; to address our students needs responsibly we must first recognize that they are unique thinkers.

Thirteen years after revealing his original theory on the seven intelligences, Gardner added an eighth intelligence, the naturalist (Gardner 1993a).

The Naturalist Intelligence

This intelligence involves outdoors-think, most closely associated with the ability to identify, categorize, and memorize the many varieties of plant and animal life. People who have a naturalist intelligence enjoy studying and interacting with animals and plants. They are our botanists, entomologists, marine biologists, and naturalists. A child who loves plants and animals, a child who enjoys learning about various species, a child who begs for pet snakes, frogs, and spiders, and who exhibits fascination with categories of other kinds (cars, airplanes, and so on), is illustrating strength in this intelligence.

How to Use This Book

I designed this book so that you can begin right away, without planning or reading anything but the MI primer and the first two or three activities in chapter 1. After this minimal preparation, you can learn along with your students. As much as possible, these lessons use few materials and facilities. The strategies assume access to standard supplies: students, classroom, desks, paper, pencils, glue, scissors, and a chalkboard and chalk or an overhead projector.

Chapter 1 sets the stage by teaching your students about MI. While it is not required that you teach these lessons before going on to the rest of the book, it will help your students and yourself to prepare them for their new learning experiences. Once they know what you are trying to accomplish with the new style of lessons, they will be more interested in their own learning styles (helpful) and less resistant to lessons (very helpful). I would schedule one half hour every day for the activities in chapter 1.

Each of chapters 2 through 9 provides a daily dose of one of the eight intelligences. I provide only a few strategies for verbal-linguistic and mathematical-logical because these intelligences already get plenty of coverage in the traditional classroom. Each chapter presents several strategies to help you use the particular intelligence more often in the classroom and apply it to *your own* curriculum.

It helps prepare students for what may be a completely unfamiliar way of learning if you take a few minutes at the beginning of a new lesson to lay the groundwork for what's coming. Each strategy starts with an overview, where you'll find a brief summary of the activities in the strategy; details about how much time each lesson takes to prepare and teach; and resources where you can review helpful information. Strategies have anywhere from one to five lessons each. Some lessons build on previous lessons, while others are independent. You may choose to do one or more lessons in a day. Most lessons include a focus period to center students before beginning, a teaching section with step-by-step instructions, a reflection section to encourage students to look back and evaluate their own learning, and an optional follow-up or extension. At the end of each lesson is a list of applications to your own curriculum for each strategy. The transfer lessons do not include step-by-step instructions, but once you have read or taught the longer lessons you can easily adapt the applications for use with your class and existing lesson plans. These transfer lessons are the most important part of each strategy. Without them, you are merely playing games (albeit enjoyable learning games) with your students, instead of using MI theory to help your students realize learning objectives and arrive at deeper levels of understanding of the lesson material and themselves.

Other than chapter 1, the chapters and strategies are not dependent on one another. You can flip through the book and find a strategy you like. You may teach these strategies in the step-by-step manner that I wrote them, or simply read the strategy, then skip the lesson and apply the strategy to your own curriculum.

How Not to Use This Book

Teachers are inundated with curricula that must be covered in the classroom. This book was *not* written to make you add *new* curricula to your load. The purpose of addressing various intelligences is not to increase subject matter to teach; it is to approach existing curricula from many perspectives, to give students better chances to learn and understand more deeply. It is so important to transfer the strategies in this book to your own, established curriculum.

Nowhere is it written that all these strategies are equally effective for all students all the time. Nor is it written that each strategy must be used in order to truly address the multiple intelligences. If any of these strategies do not appear to add to the learning experiences of your students, then set those strategies aside. I would hate to see a teacher continue to use a strategy that shows no learning value.

An unfortunate side effect of using MI theory in the classroom is a new kind of labeling or pigeon-holing of students, in which a particular student is designated as having only one or two intelligences: This student is visual, that one is physical. This labeling counteracts the primary purpose of using MI theory—to *increase* students' available learning avenues.

Now Get Started!

Use this book to give your students the necessary space and tools to be who they are and to grow every day. MI theory provides us with a wonderful framework for addressing and aiding the various brains sitting in front of us in the classroom. It should not be used to limit our students' possibilities, but rather to expand their capacities.

1

Setting the Stage

The activities in this chapter introduce your students and you to the basics of multiple intelligence theory. These nine lessons will help you acquire information about your students' proclivities, and your students will begin to focus and take responsibility for their own learning styles. They will begin to appreciate learning differences among their classmates, and your class will become receptive to

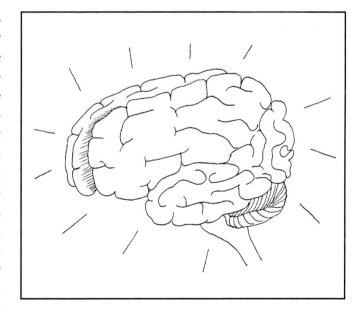

various intelligences and styles of learning, which will make introducing the multiple intelligence lessons easier. After completing the activities here, your students and you will have the information you need to use the rest of the learning strategies in this book.

Activity 1

Portfolios and Thought Journals

In Brief

Based on examples you provide, students create personal portfolios for storing their thoughts and any information they find on thinking and the brain.

Time

25 minutes (includes 10 minutes prep time)

Objectives

To set the stage for the introduction of multiple intelligence activities

To provide students with journals in which to write, draw, and keep other records of their experiences with multiple intelligence lessons

Background

This initial activity and others in the chapter gradually introduce students to a brand new way of thinking and learning. As students progress through the multiple intelligence activities, they will use the portfolio to track their growth and store their learning.

Learning Approaches

visual-spatial (copying what you see)

bodily-kinesthetic (hand-eye coordination)

Materials

one sheet per student of large construction paper

staplers and staples

notebook paper or composition books

blank drawing paper

example portfolios

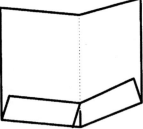

Preparation

Before starting this activity, create three to five example portfolios as models. The portfolios should include construction paper folders with pockets for extra papers, articles, and so on, and thought journals, with lined and blank pages (approximately ten to fifteen pages each).

Teach

Step 1: Tell students they will be creating folders that they'll use to collect notes, sketches, and work sheets as they learn about the human brain and their own thinking and learning processes.

Step 2: Show students the example portfolios you prepared and explain that they can use the examples for ideas but that they are not required to copy what they see.

Step 3: Either set the materials and example portfolios at an activity center where individual students or partners can look at the example and make their own, or divide the class into groups and provide each group with materials and one example portfolio.

Step 4: Give students five to ten minutes to work. When they're done, ask them to label the outside of their portfolios with their names and the title "A Place for My Thoughts."

Reflect

Challenge students to continue to collect items of interest to store in their thought journals. Ask them, "What kinds of things could you collect about the brain? Where could you look for these things?" Accept and discuss any answers: photographs; information they learn from their parents, friends, movies, or television; information from books or posters about the brain; and so on.

Follow-up and Extension

Invite students to add to their portfolios whenever they choose (articles, drawings, their own written ideas about thinking, and so on). Periodically, collect the portfolios and review them to check student progress and to note student interests to guide you in collecting classroom references.

Activity 2

Thinking and My Brain

In Brief

In order to focus their attention and interest, students make lists of what they already know and what they want to find out about learning and the brain.

Time

20 minutes

Objective

To encourage students to generate questions about thinking and how their brains function

Background

This lesson is designed to spark students' interest in the human brain and their own thought processes. This exercise will provide the first entry in their thought journals, and it is an activity that you can return to in order to check learning as the unit progresses.

Learning Approaches

verbal-linguistic (use of words)

intrapersonal (self-reflection)

Materials

thought journals

Focus

Ask, "Who wants to guarantee that they remember what they learn in this class?" Explain that scientific research shows that people who ask questions about a subject before they start to learn remember more of their learning than those who don't ask questions. Ask students to guess why this phenomenon might be true.

Teach

Step 1: Have students divide the first page of their journals into two columns, the first titled "What I know about thinking and my brain," and the second, "What I want to know about thinking and my brain." Draw example columns on the chalkboard or overhead projector.

Step 2: Through class discussion, generate one or two items for each column. Then give students ten minutes to work independently to come up with several more statements and questions.

What I Know about Thinking	What I Wonder about Thinking
1. thinking happens in my brain	1. Do I think when I sleep?
2. my brain connects to my body with nerves	2. How does my brain work?
3. animals can't think like people	3. Can a brain grow?
4.	4.
5.	5.

Step 3: Ask for volunteers to share what they wrote.

Step 4: Explain that the class will be learning about thinking and the brain. Explain that they can add more to column 2 if they think of additional questions, but they must leave column 1 alone for future comparisons.

Follow-up and Extension

As the unit progresses, schedule class time for students to refer back to their charts as their questions are answered and as they think of new questions.

Did You Know?

Students who generate their own questions before studying a subject retain more information and learn to seek more answers than those who don't ask questions (Jensen 1994a, 135).

Activity 3

Thinking about the Ways We Think

In Brief

Students examine images from magazines, newspapers, catalogs, and so on and discuss whether and what kinds of thinking and learning are taking place. Discussion about the nature of thinking will help some students arrive at the idea that thinking takes place all the time, while others may try to limit the scope of what defines thinking.

Time

30 minutes (includes 5 minutes prep time)

Objectives

To foster student recognition that thinking permeates all parts of our lives: work, play, and school

To help students understand that people are constantly involved with learning and that learning happens in many ways

Background

By first understanding that thinking takes place in all human activity, students will readily grasp the multiple intelligence categories.

Learning Approaches

interpersonal (group discussion)
visual-spatial (collage)

Materials

glue
scissors
6 to 7 copies of a brain drawing
old catalogs and magazines
construction paper

Preparation

Bring in old magazines, newspapers, catalogs, and other materials with lots of pictures that can be cut up.

Focus

Explain to students that they will be working in groups. Review with them the following rules of acceptable group behavior (you may make a poster for the classroom).

- Stay in your group.

- Work together.

- Discuss what you find with your partners.

- Work quietly.

- Do not put down others' thoughts and ideas.

Important! Students who feel unsafe expressing ideas will stop trying. Encourage discussion and debate without put-downs!

Teach

Step 1: Write the following prompts on the board:

- This person is thinking and learning by

  _____ .

- These people are thinking and learning by

  _____ .

- I think and learn by

  _____ .

Step 2: Say, "Scientists have been learning a great deal about the brain. For instance, the brain can think and learn in many ways. In fact, certain parts of our brains are assigned specific jobs. Today we are going to try to guess some of the many ways in which people think and learn."

Step 3: Divide the class into groups of four or five and explain that they'll be making collages about thinking. Each group needs glue, scissors, one piece of construction paper, and magazines and other materials.

Step 4: Ask students to work together. Tell them to do the following:

- Paste the large picture of the brain onto the group's piece of construction paper.

- Work individually to find and cut out pictures of people who they believe are thinking and learning.

- Share the pictures with their groups. For each picture an individual has, she completes the statements on the board.

- After everyone has found some pictures of people thinking and learning, make a collage by pasting all the pictures onto the poster around the brain.

Step 5: Say, "Your group should look for various kinds of thinking. If you cannot find a picture to represent a special way of thinking that you come up with, write it down as a sentence on your poster. For example, 'I think about the sky when I am swinging on a swing.'"

Step 6: Give students fifteen minutes to work on their collages while you walk around and listen to group discussions about thinking. Compliment students on their use of the prompts or any creative ideas, particularly any discussion about thinking that takes place. For instance, I had one student say, "That isn't thinking; they are playing a game," and another student answer, "That is, too, thinking—they have to decide what to do or learn how to swing the bat!"

Follow-up and Extension

Encourage students to collect in their portfolios photos and lists of things they like to do, are good at doing, and would like to learn how to do.

Activity 4

Ways of Thinking

In Brief

Students sort their pictures according to the eight intelligences. Once they understand the categories, they will add more activities to each group.

Time

27 minutes (includes 2 minutes prep time)

Objective

To introduce students to the categories of thinking established in multiple intelligence theory

Background

This lesson has students sort the pictures of learning and thinking from the previous activity. By categorizing the pictures, students start to see the relationships among the various ways of thinking. This activity leads up to activity 5, in which students will make up names for the categories of thinking.

Learning Approaches

verbal-linguistic (use of words)

mathematical-logical and naturalist (grouping, sorting)

Materials

students' collages from activity 3

Teach

Step 1: Ask each group to share its collage and to report and explain the different thinking and learning activities they noticed.

Step 2: As each group names an activity depicted in its collage, write it on the chalkboard or overhead projector, grouping the activities based on the eight intelligences. Do not label the groups; simply make sure each is distinct from the rest. It's okay for some activities to fall into two or more categories (for example, cooking might use bodily-kinesthetic, naturalist, and mathematical-logical intelligences).

Step 3: Once students understand the sorting pattern, allow them to expand the lists.

Step 4: Copy the list down once it's complete, because you will use it in the next activity.

2
- drawing
- seeing pictures in your head
- looking at pictures
- watching movies
- studying and drawing maps
- doing jigsaw puzzles

3
- playing sports
- acting
- signing language
- playing roles
- moving around
- using and interpreting body language
- dancing
- cooking
- performing

1
- singing songs
- playing instruments
- reading music
- making up a rap
- listening to music
- tapping
- enjoying sounds

8
- categorizing
- recognizing similarities and differences
- interacting with nature
- collecting
- observing closely
- focusing attention
- enjoying pets

7
- daydreaming
- pondering
- thinking alone
- inventing
- doing solo activities
- guessing
- feeling instincts
- examining own thoughts and feelings

4
- showing interest in numbers
- doing puzzles
- solving problems
- charting
- graphing

6
- working in groups
- playing team sports
- cooperating
- helping others
- teaching
- conversing

5
- showing interest in words
- reading
- writing
- spelling
- understanding vocabulary
- listening to stories
- giving speeches

Follow-up and Extension

Put the lists of activities on a classroom poster and encourage students to think of more ideas to add to the lists at future dates.

Activity 5

Naming the Eight Intelligences

In Brief

Students work in small groups to come up with names for the learning categories they discovered in activity 4.

Time

25 to 40 minutes (includes 5 to 20 minutes prep time)

Objective

To teach students the categories of intelligence set forth in multiple intelligence theory

Background

By making up their own names for the intelligences, students will better understand the meaning of the official labels.

Learning Approaches

verbal-linguistic (use of words)

mathematical-logical and naturalist (grouping, sorting)

Ninety-nine percent of learning is not on any conscious level. Students are listening and learning from everything around them: your tone of voice, your body language, the periphery sounds and sights. Try displaying posters in your classroom that are relevant to your teaching (Jensen 1994a).

Materials

the lists from activity 4 copied onto the chalkboard or an overhead projector

a poster that lists the eight intelligences

Preparation

Make a poster for the classroom that lists the eight intelligences on the left hand side, with room on the right for symbols and labels the students will create.

Teach

Step 1: Divide the class into eight groups. Assign each group one list. Explain that these lists correspond to intelligences. Ask each group to think of a label or title for their assigned list of activities. Give them five to seven minutes to decide on the labels.

Step 2: Have each group choose a reporter to present the list and titles and explain how the titles cover all activities on the list.

Step 3: Write their ideas onto the chalkboard or overhead projector. Examples are shown on page 21.

Step 4: Display the poster that lists the eight intelligences. Explain to students that this list was designed by Howard Gardner about ten years ago. Explain that the list isn't necessarily complete and that more thinking and learning styles might be discovered as more is learned about how the brain works. (I always say, "Maybe one of you will grow up to be the pioneer who makes the next big discovery about our brains!")

Step 5: Vote as a class on the best student labels and add them to the poster.

Follow-up and Extension

Ask students to work in small groups to develop a symbol for each of the intelligences. Add their symbols to the poster.

Student Ideas for Titles

2   Seeing

- drawing
- seeing pictures in your head
- looking at pictures
- watching movies
- studying and drawing maps
- doing jigsaw puzzles

3   Body

- playing sports
- acting
- signing language
- playing roles
- moving around
- using and interpreting body language
- dancing
- cooking
- performing

1   Music

- singing songs
- playing instruments
- reading music
- making up a rap
- listening to music
- tapping
- enjoying sounds

8   Nature

- categorizing
- recognizing similarities and differences
- interacting with nature
- collecting
- observing closely
- focusing attention
- enjoying pets

7   Wondering

- daydreaming
- pondering
- thinking alone
- inventing
- doing solo activities
- guessing
- feeling instincts
- examining own thoughts and feelings

4   Numbers

- showing interest in numbers
- doing puzzles
- solving problems
- charting
- graphing

6   Teams

- working in groups
- playing team sports
- cooperating
- helping others
- teaching
- conversing

5   Words

- showing interest in words
- reading
- writing
- spelling
- understanding vocabulary
- listening to stories
- giving speeches

Activity 6

My Own Thinking Map

In Brief

Students draw pictures and write sentences about activities they enjoy or perform well. They then connect those statements and symbols to a chart of the eight intelligences.

Time

25 minutes (includes 5 minutes prep time)

Objective

To foster students' awareness of their varying capabilities within the multiple intelligence framework

Background

This lesson encourages students to examine their own interests and skills and associates those interests and skills with the eight intelligences. Students will begin to appreciate the role the intelligences play in their lives.

Learning Approaches

verbal-linguistic (use of words)

visual-spatial (drawing)

intrapersonal (self-reflection)

Materials

one copy for each student of My Own Thinking Map work sheet

thought journals

Preparation

Make copies of My Own Thinking Map work sheet.

Teach

Step 1: Pass out work sheets, tell students to do the following steps, and make sure students understand what they are supposed to do.

- Write down things they like to do.

- Draw symbols for things they like to do.

- Write down things they are good at.

- Draw symbols for things they are good at.

- Write down things they want to learn.

- Draw symbols for things they want to learn.

Step 2: Have students draw lines and arrows connecting each item to one or two of the eight intelligences on the work sheet. Give students about fifteen minutes to complete the work sheet.

Step 3: This activity is the first where students begin to look at their own learning styles and preferences. Some may find their sheets weighted in one or two areas, others may find themselves balanced across the spectrum. Explain that either of these situations is fine, and that there are no right answers. You may want to wander the room, discuss student findings, and ask questions.

Step 4: Students may say such things as "I like to cook; which intelligence does that use?" Encourage them to find an answer by asking, "Well, what exactly is it about cooking that you like?" Some will say the smell and the act of making the food (bodily-kinesthetic); others will say working with recipes and measurements (verbal and mathematical); still others will point out that they like the "look of food" (visual-spatial). Allow them the freedom to explore the many intelligences involved in any one activity.

Follow-up and Extension

Collect these papers to review. It gives you a chance to see how your students see themselves. Return them and ask students to store the work sheets in their thought journals for future reference.

Activity 7

Efficient Brains

In Brief

By working different mazes and learning about some brain research, students learn that a brain that is strong in all of its parts has access to more problem-solving strategies. Therefore, it has more pathways to solve problems quickly.

Name: _____

In the blank areas around the picture below, draw, write, or paste pictures of things you like to do, things you are good at doing, and things you would like to learn to do. Then connect each activity with arrows to the intelligences it uses most.

Verbal/Linguistic

Naturalist

Intrapersonal

Physical/Kinesthetic

Interpersonal

Musical/Rhythmic

Mathematical/Logical

$x + y = z$

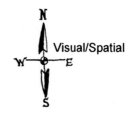
Visual/Spatial

Multliple Intelligences Made Easy © 1999 Zephyr Press, Inc., Tucson, Arizona

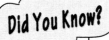

Did You Know?
Neurons (cells in the brain) grow branchlike connections called *dendrites.* These branches reach out and form the pathways that our brains use to think.

Time

35 minutes (includes 10 minutes prep time)

Objective

To teach students that a brain that is well developed in all intelligences has more pathways and can work more quickly and effectively than a brain that is not developed in all intelligences

Background

Using the analogy of pathways in the brain helps students understand how a well-developed brain has several options and ways to arrive at a given destination. We know the intelligences are interrelated and work in concert. In *Creating Minds,* Gardner observes that many of the geniuses of the twentieth century (Albert Einstein, Pablo Picasso, and Igor Stravinsky, to name a few) used a perspective from outside their usual disciplines to arrive at some of their greatest discoveries and achievements. For instance, Einstein visualized (visual-spatial) the act of traveling on a light beam many times before he developed his theory of the speed of light (mathematical-logical.) This activity connects the MI concept of using many pathways for learning with the results of scientific research that shows how the brain works when it solves problems. The research shows that some brains work more efficiently than others. This strategy proposes that by working the many areas of the brain a person develops a more efficient brain.

Learning Approaches

visual-spatial (pictures, images, visual puzzles)

mathematical-logical (puzzles, measurements, and logic)

Materials

rulers or string (which can make measuring more intriguing)

one copy for each student of Brain Mazes work sheet

Preparation

Make copies of the Brain Mazes work sheet. Make an overhead of brains A and B or copy them onto the chalkboard.

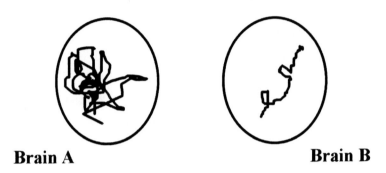

Brain A   **Brain B**

Teach

Step 1: Tell the following story.

In an experiment, scientists were trying to find out what a really good brain looks like when it is hard at work. They used special machines to take pictures of brains at work. In one experiment, these scientists asked a number of people to take a difficult problem-solving test. The scientists photographed these people's brains while the people worked on solving the problems. The scientists got a variety of results, but one thing they noticed was that some of the brains, such as brain A, were very active all over, and some, such as brain B, were less active.

Step 2: Ask students, "Which brains do you think did better on the test and why?" Allow students to answer and hypothesize why. Don't comment except to say, "That's an interesting hypothesis."

Step 3: Pass out copies of the work sheet, read the instructions, make sure students understand them, and give students fifteen minutes to complete the mazes.

Step 4: After students have completed the work sheet, ask them to look again at the two brains on the chalkboard or overhead. Ask students to think about what they might have learned from doing the work sheet. Then ask them which brain they think performed better on the tests.

Step 5: Tell students that brain B scored much higher on the tests. Ask them, "Why do you think the second brain scored better?" Students should understand that this brain had to do less work to make the necessary connections because there were more pathways. (Your students may devise other theories about why those showing less activity scored well. Accept any logical hypotheses and explain that as yet we can only theorize.)

Step 6: Ask students, "Do you think a brain that is well developed and balanced in all of its areas would have more connections and pathways, or fewer?"

Follow-up and Extension

Have students look up the word *efficient* and explain what it has to do with the two brain types. On another day ask a student volunteer to retell the story of the two brain types. Make sure the student (or other members of the class) can remember why the brains that showed less activity were more successful on the test.

Activity 8

Brain Parts

In Brief

You demonstrate that two fists held fingers to fingers can be used as a brain model. Students label their hands with parts of the brain using a handout as a guide.

Time

25 minutes (includes 5 minutes prep time)

Objectives

To teach students basic brain anatomy

To show the primary areas that govern the intelligences

Background

This lesson teaches students the areas of the brain that govern the various intelligences. Students see that by developing all their intelligences they will strengthen all areas of their brains. By using fists as models, you will be able to refer to the brain parts easily in future lessons as students move on to learning how to use and develop their intelligences.

Learning Approaches

verbal-linguistic (use of words)

interpersonal (working in pairs)

bodily-kinesthetic (using the body, acting out)

Name: _____

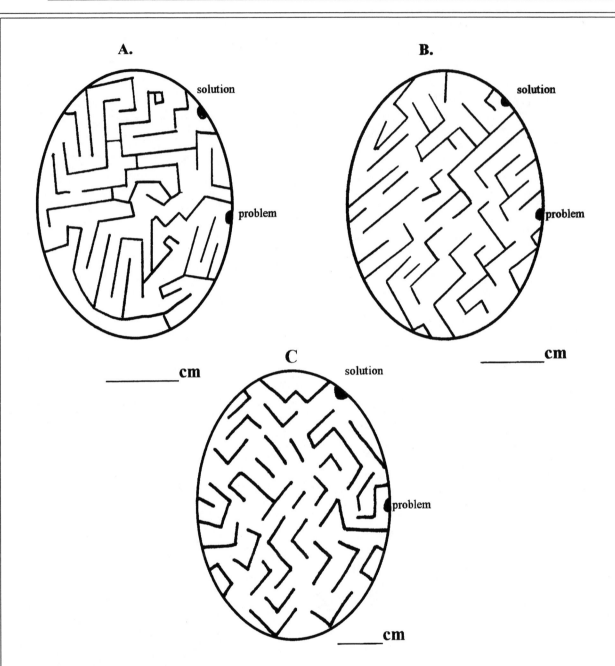

A.

solution

problem

_____ cm

B.

solution

problem

_____ cm

C

solution

problem

_____ cm

Find the path from the problems to the solutions in mazes A, B, and C. Then use a ruler (and some string if you have it) to measure the paths. Answer the questions that follow.

1. Which path is the longest? _____ Shortest? _____

2. Which maze was easiest to solve? _____ Why? _____

_____

Multliple Intelligences Made Easy © 1999 Zephyr Press, Inc., Tucson, Arizona

Materials

one copy for each student of Brain Parts handouts or two overhead transparencies

ten blank sticky labels or strips of masking tape for each student

Preparation

Make copies of the Brain Parts handout on pages 30–31 or make two overhead transparencies.

Teach

Step 1: Tell students, "Today we are going to learn a little about the parts of our brains and the jobs assigned to each part."

Step 2: Ask students to look at the overhead transparency or their handouts and follow along as you point out the brain parts.

Step 3: Ask students to make fists as brain models and give them ten minutes to label these models using the stickers. Students can work in pairs and each label a partner's fists or, if no stickers are available, each student can point to the various brain parts on the partner's hands.

Step 4: Tell students that as you begin to do multiple intelligence activities you will refer back to their hand models to see which brain parts are being worked.

Follow-up and Extension

Refer to the hand model as you go through the lessons in this book so that students will remember they are working to develop various parts of their brains. Set up a learning center of brain books, graphics, and models so that students can learn more about the brain's anatomy. (Launa Ellison's [1995] *The Brain: A User's Guide* is a good resource.)

Activity 9

Star Brains

In Brief

Via a connect-the-dots exercise, students learn that multiple intelligence lessons exercise various parts of the brain at once and the brains become stronger and more efficient.

Time

15 minutes

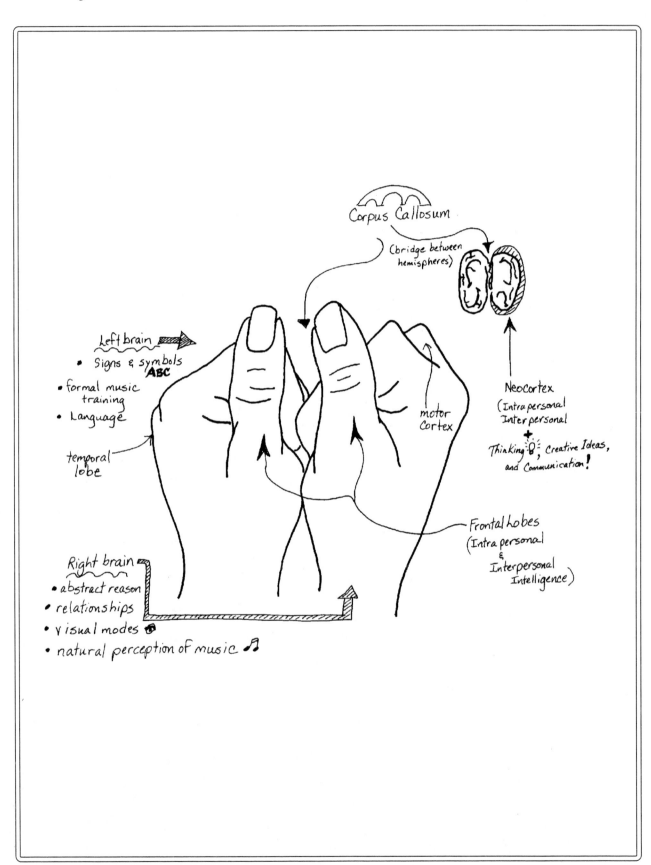

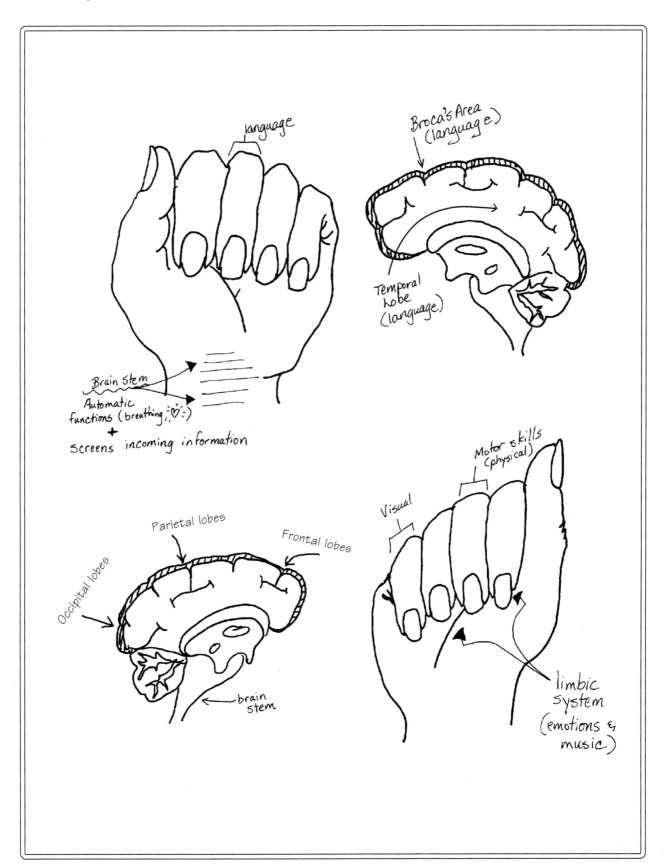

language

Broca's Area
(language)

Temporal
lobe
(language)

Brain Stem

Automatic
functions (breathing, ♡ :)
+
Screens incoming information

Parietal lobes

Occipital lobes

Frontal lobes

brain
stem

Motor skills
(physical)

Visual

limbic
System
(emotions &
music)

Objective

To help students understand the importance of using various approaches when learning

Background

This lesson prepares students for the exercises in this book by explaining that you plan to use various intelligences so that all their brain areas are developed and used.

Learning Approaches

verbal-linguistic (use of words)

visual-spatial (design)

Materials

thought journals

Teach

Step 1: Say to students, "We've learned a little about how the brain works and about the various intelligences we have. Can anyone remember some of the seven ways we think and learn?"

Step 2: As students name intelligences, draw dots in a circle on the chalkboard and label each with the name of an intelligence. Ask students to copy your example on blank pieces of paper in their thought journals.

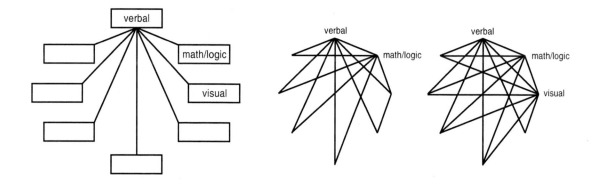

Step 3: Say to students, "Now let's talk about something we do in school. Can anyone name an activity we do that has to do with the verbal-linguistic intelligence?" Suggest that they look at their personal intelligence charts for ideas.

Step 4: As students name verbal-linguistic activities, draw lines from that point to all other intelligences that are served by the activities (see illustration). Say, "Remember how we learned that our brains work better if we make the pathways in our brains strong so our brains have a lot of different choices? Well, when we use multiple intelligence strategies to teach verbal-linguistic skills such as the ones you named, we strengthen other parts of our brains and open pathways like these lines I'm drawing."

Step 5: Ask students to name school activities that use the mathematical-logical intelligence. Ask a student volunteer to draw on the chalkboard the lines from point 2 to all the other points. Ask, "Why is (student) drawing these lines? What do the lines show about what's happening in our brains when we use multiple intelligence techniques to learn math?"

Step 6: Ask what needs to happen for the picture to turn into a star. Pause and let students think. Encourage them to understand that all lines have to be drawn to all points, or that all the intelligence areas have to be worked.

Step 7: Repeat step 5 with each of the remaining intelligences, each time asking a different student to draw the line and explain why. Make sure before you end the lesson that all students understand that using multiple intelligences in the classroom will help them build bigger and better learning pathways in their brains.

Step 8: Say to students, "Look, our finished picture looks like a star! When we use all our intelligences instead of just two or three, our brains will look and act like stars."

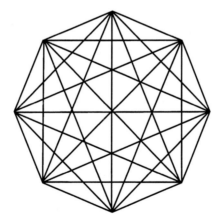

Reflect

Ask students if they are prepared to turn their brains into Star Brains and what they think that term means. Allow students to copy and color the star design in their thought journals and write a few words about what it teaches them. Explain that you will be trying out special teaching activities every day to develop all their ways of thinking.

2

Musical-Rhythmic Intelligence

This book begins with strategies for enhancing the musical-rhythmic intelligence because it is perhaps one of the least used intelligences in the traditional elementary curriculum. Music is generally used as enrichment, only taught by a specialist for one hour a week. Some teachers may introduce a few songs during the school year and have holiday music programs, but regular exposure to music is rare. This chapter provides six ways to use music for more than talent enrichment; these strategies use music to teach subject matter by associating the qualities and elements of music with the information being learned.

REMINDER

Learning by using music will probably be completely foreign to many of your students. As you teach the lessons in this chapter, preview each one with your students by summarizing the activities and goals.

Incorporating music into the classroom on a regular basis has great rewards. Students love to listen to all kinds of music. Music can calm, excite, motivate, and even increase math abilities. Students who are seldom successful with other learning approaches may come to life when you offer a musical approach.

Beyond the strategies in this book, I highly recommend playing classical music in the classroom while students are working. Use music to identify transition periods or group work. Use music to relax students who have just returned from the playground. Use music to soothe nervous tension right before a test or presentation. Use music of particular time periods to match your history unit.

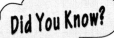

Did You Know?

Studies show that students who listen regularly to Mozart increase their math abilities.*

REMINDER

Students are going to want to perform any songs they create, not turn them in on paper. They also like to be recognized for the work they put into their creations. Consider staging classroom Grammy Awards each time you use a musical strategy. As their example, you need to act out, sing, express, snap your fingers, and generally ham it up when you use these techniques. The more you have fun, the more energy your students will put into their songs.

* For more information about the ongoing research into music's effect on learning, see the *Musica Newsletter*, edited by Norman Weinberger, Center for Neurobiology and Memory, University of California at Irvine, Irvine, CA 92717-3800. You can also check out the website at http://www.musica.uci.edu.

Strategy 1

Choral Writing

In Brief

Students first learn how the musical components of repetition, rhythm and rhyme, and expressive phrasing make material interesting to listen to, hence easier to learn and remember. They then transform written learning materials into original choral compositions, using the strategies of rhythm and rhyme to make their own study materials more interesting.

Objective

To teach students how to organize, recite, and recall information through the use of musical repetition, rhythm and rhyme, and expressive phrases

Background

When students are encouraged to create these kinds of choral readings, the results can be exciting and powerful. The first choral reading I heard was a class performing a series of essays about Martin Luther King Jr. Various groups read various parts of the essays, and the pieces were intertwined in a kind of symphony of words that juxtaposed the essays in a new and thought-provoking way.

Lesson 1: Learning through Repetition

Time

40 minutes (includes 10 minutes prep time)

Materials

one copy for each student of Choral Writing work sheet
students' social studies or science textbooks

Preparation

Make copies of the Choral Writing work sheet. Gather ideas from textbook for step 6. Divide students into groups of three or four.

Focus

Ask students to recall a song with repetition ("This Old Man" and "If You're Happy and You Know It" are two good examples). Ask them,

"Which lines of the song are easiest to remember? Why?" Encourage them to understand that the repetition of the chorus in each song engraves it on their memories.

Teach

Step 1: Ask students to listen carefully while you read the following passage. Let them know that you will read it only once.

The rainbow color of a dragonfly's body and its netted wings are admired all around the world. It is hard to believe these delicate creatures are one of the few survivors of the prehistoric age. The ancestors of dragonflies lived almost 300 million years ago, before the time of dinosaurs. Fossil records show scientists that the dragonfly has changed very little, except in size. The early dragonflies were giants! Their wings sometimes stretched thirty inches, tip to tip. They had the same large eyes and pointy bodies as the dragonflies of today, but today dragonflies seldom grow larger than five to seven inches.

Step 2: Allow the small groups five minutes to work together to answer the questions in section 1 of the work sheet.

Step 3: Ask students to listen carefully again as you read the following passage; remind them that you will read the passage only once.

The dragonfly, queen of the air, shiny shell and netted wings.
All over the world, it has lived.
300 million years, it has lived.
The dragonfly lived long ago, before the dinosaur.
Its body has remained the same, the fossils show.
All over the world, it has lived.
300 million years, it has lived.
The dragonfly from years ago grew big, like arms spread wide.
Today it looks just the same, but fits into a hand.
All over the world, it has lived.
300 million years, it has lived.

Step 4: Allow groups seven to ten minutes to discuss and answer sections 2 and 3 of the work sheet.

Step 5: Ask a reporter from each group to share with the class her group's answers for section 3 of the work sheet. List all groups' answers on the chalkboard or overhead.

Step 6: Ask students individually or in their groups to choose a paragraph from their textbook to rewrite using repetition to highlight the piece of information they consider to be the most important or most interesting. Stress that there are no right or wrong answers for this project.

Step 7: After about ten or fifteen minutes, ask each group or student to share the results for the class to enjoy.

Reflect

Ask a student volunteer to summarize what he noticed and learned from this activity. Ask students to make notes in their thought journal about one idea or thought they get from this activity.

Lesson 2: Rhyme and Reason

Time

40 minutes (includes 10 minutes prep time)

Materials

one copy for each student of Choral Writing work sheet
social studies or science text

Preparation

Make copies of the Choral Writing work sheet. Look through textbook unit to gather ideas for step 6. Divide class into groups of three or four.

Focus

Ask students to recall a nursery rhyme (for example "Humpty Dumpty" or "Mary Had a Little Lamb"). Ask them, "What do you think makes it so easy to remember nursery rhymes even when you haven't said them for years?" Students should realize that rhythm and rhyme play a role in memory.

Teach

Step 1: Ask students to listen carefully while you read the following only once:

Dragonflies go through a three-stage metamorphosis. They begin life as **eggs** *that are laid in fresh-water ponds and streams. After about one week, the eggs hatch into* **nymphs**. *They spend this second stage underwater, as well. Nymphs do not have wings and they grow very quickly. As they grow they shed old outer shells that are too small. This process is called* **molting**. *After molting many times the nymph is ready for the third life-stage. The nymph crawls out of the water and rests somewhere. It allows the sun to dry out its outer shell. When the shell dries, it cracks open. The adult dragonfly crawls out. It spreads its new wings and lives the rest of its life out of water.*

Strategy 1 Work Sheet

Choral Writing

Name: _____

Section 1

What do you and your group members remember from the first passage?

What was easiest to remember?

Why?

Section 2

What do you and your group members remember from the second passage?

What was easiest to remember?

Why?

Section 3

Compare the two passages. What is similar? Different?

Which passage is easier to remember and think about?

Why?

Step 2: Allow the small groups five minutes to work together to answer the questions in section 1 of the work sheet.

Step 3: Ask students to listen carefully again as you read the following passage; remind them that you will read the passage only once.

> *In a three stage metamorphosis—*
> *That is how the dragonflies exist.*
> *They change two times:*
> *Egg to nymph,*
> *Nymph to fly,*
> *In a three stage metamorphosis.*
> *The dragonfly lays eggs in ponds and streams;*
> *They crack and the second life-stage begins*
> *Nymphs crawl in the water and they grow and molt their shells*
> *So their third life-stage can soon begin.*
> *To become an adult fly*
> *The nymph must crawl up high*
> *Out of water so the sun can make*
> *It's hard shell dry.*
> *When it molts this last time,*
> *The nymph has wings and now can fly.*
> *In a three stage metamorphosis—*
> *That is how the dragonflies exist.*
> *They change two times:*
> *Egg to nymph,*
> *Nymph to fly,*
> *In a three stage metamorphosis.*

Step 4: Allow groups seven to ten minutes to discuss and answer sections 2 and 3 of the work sheet.

Step 5: Ask a reporter from each group to share with the class his group's answers for section 3 of the work sheet. List all the groups' answers on the chalkboard or overhead.

Step 6: Ask students individually or in their groups to choose a paragraph from their textbook to rewrite using repetition to highlight the piece of information they consider to be the most important or most interesting. Stress that there are no right or wrong answers for this project. Suggest that they turn to the chapter review and pick two or three facts to rewrite into a simple rhyme. Challenge students to do extensive rhymes if they think they can.

Step 7: After about fifteen minutes, ask each group or student to share the results for the class to enjoy. Do not require all students to perform; some students may not finish their rhymes.

Reflect

Ask a student volunteer to summarize what he or she noticed and learned from this activity.

Lesson 3: Express Yourself

Time

40 minutes (includes 5 minutes prep time)

Materials

one copy for each student of Choral Writing work sheet
social studies or science text

Preparation

Make copies of the Choral Writing work sheet. Divide class into groups of three or four.

Focus

Ask students to think of some verbal expressions that communicate a feeling ("Aha!" "Wow!" and "Yuck!" are all good ones).

Teach

Step 1: Ask students to listen carefully while you read the following passage only once.

*Adult dragonflies and their nymphs are predators. They use their great eyesight to help them hunt and survive. They catch and eat other insects. Nymphs eat baby mosquitoes, tadpoles, and even small fish. Dragonflies eat other flying bugs such as mosquitoes and gnats. They both have large lower lips (**labia**) that extend to catch their prey. Adult dragonflies catch their prey while in flight. They chew the food with their mandibles (jaws), and clean off their eye lenses with their legs. Then off they fly to find more prey.*

Step 2: Allow the small groups five minutes to answer the questions in section 1 of the work sheet.

Step 3: Ask students to listen carefully again as you read the following passage with a lot of expression and emphasis in your voice; remind them that you will read the passage only once.

*Dragonflies hunt; they're gr-e-e-eat **hunters!***

Catching mosquitoes and gnat-nat-nats.

*Even Nymphs are gre-e-eat **hunters!***

*Catching baby mosquitoes, **tad**poles, and little bitty fish.*

*Dragonflies and nymphs have terrific **eyes** that see all directions,*

*Then out comes their bottom lip and **snatch!** they have their prey!*

They chew their food, and clean their eyes, and off they go to catch some more . . . mmm . . . mmmm . . . mmmm.

Step 4: Allow groups seven to ten minutes to discuss and answer sections 2 and 3 of the work sheet.

Step 5: Ask a reporter from each group to share with the class his group's answers for section 3 of the work sheet. List all the groups' answers on the chalkboard or overhead.

Step 6: Ask students individually or in their groups to choose a paragraph from their textbook to rewrite using expressive phrases to emphasize the most important or most interesting piece.

Step 7: After about fifteen minutes, ask each group or student to share the results for the class to enjoy.

Reflect

Ask a student volunteer to summarize what she noticed and learned from this activity.

Lesson 4: All Together Now

Time

40 minutes (includes 5 minutes prep time)

Materials

one copy for each student of Choral Writing work sheet

students' social studies or science textbook, or some other current class reading material

Preparation

From current reading material, choose five passages that lend themselves to choral writing.

Focus

Tell students that the rewriting they have been doing can be called *choral writing*. Remind them that when they added elements usually found only in music to the written information, it made the material more interesting and easier to remember. Explain that the novelty of the sound and the musicality help us recall and understand the information better. Ask students to name the elements that are helpful to choral writing (repetition, rhythm and rhyme, and expressive phrases). Write the three elements on the chalkboard or overhead.

Teach

Step 1: Explain that the class is going to learn how to put all these elements together, starting with a relatively simple example.

Step 2: Ask students to open their textbooks to one of the less complex passages you chose. Pick a group of students to be the chorus and four or five students each to be soloists. Ask the chorus to find the sentence that expresses the main idea in the passage, which they can use as it is or rewrite with simpler words. Assign each of the soloists one of the detail sentences from the passage.

Step 3: Ask the choral group to read aloud the chorus sentence in unison. After each recitation of the chorus, one of the soloists should read a detail sentence. Following is an example passage.

*Dragonflies and their cousins, damselflies, have many interesting body features. In some species the outer covering has an iridescent glow. This effect is caused by a layer of liquid under the outer shell and the wings. Sunlight reflects off the liquid causing the metallic color. The colors of dragonflies help them find the right mate. Dragonfly eyes are very large, taking up most of the head. Dragonflies are able to see sideways, behind and ahead all at the same time. Their thorax (middle) contains gills for breathing underwater when they are in the nymph stage. As they become adults, the thorax develops breathing holes called **spiracles**. Their abdomens are long and pointed, almost as if they have a very large stinger. They do not sting, but have been known to bite.*

Following is part of the simple choral writing of the passage:

Chorus: *Dragonflies have . . . oooooh . . . neat bodies.*
Solo 1: *In some species the shell has an iridescent glow.*
Chorus
Solo 2: *This effect is caused by a layer of liquid under the shell and the wings.*
Chorus
Solo 3: *Sunlight reflects off the liquid causing the metallic color.*

Step 4: Divide the class into small groups or pairs. Assign each group a paragraph from one of the current textbooks. Ask them to create a choral writing based on their assigned paragraphs, using whatever combination of repetition, rhyme and rhythm, and expressive phrasing that they think works best.

Step 5: Schedule performances so the groups can share their efforts.

Reflect

Ask students to evaluate the choral writing technique. Ask the class to volunteer answers to these questions: "In what ways do you like it better than simply reading through material? In what ways is it more difficult?" Ask students, "When would be the best time to use this technique?" Encourage them to see that choral writing is a good way to add more novelty and interest to new subject matter, as well as an exciting way to review material and retain more information before a test.

REMINDER Before starting a new choral writing assignment, always refresh students' memory by asking for the elements of choral writing: repetition, rhythm and rhyme, and expression.

Follow-up and Extension

Allow students to use choral writing to rewrite classroom or school rules. Have a Grammy Awards ceremony, with categories including "Most Effective at Teaching the Rules," "Most Entertaining," and "Most Musical."

Applying the Strategy to Curriculum

Note: Keep in mind that it isn't as important that the songs are perfect as it is that the students are engaged in arranging and composing the information.

Use choral writing for any of the following:

- as a homework assignment when you want students to review material

- as an enjoyable group method for reviewing material (combine choral writing with the jigsaw strategy in chapter 5 for an even more engaging way to review lessons)

- as part of a lesson on finding the main idea in any topic

- as a pick-me-up or novelty to retain or regain class interest in otherwise dry material

Science

1. As a class, assign special sound effects to each important step in a scientific process the class is studying. Assign each noise to a student and ask students to make the noises each time their part of the process is mentioned. Following are some examples:

   "WHOOSH! the magnets pull together when opposites come face to face!"

   "'Le-et the sun shine, oh le-et the sun shine in!' sings the chlorophyll that makes sun into food."

2. Dry science textbooks are excellent fodder for choral writing. For any passage, give the challenge: "Can you find a way to use rhythm, repetition, and expression to make the main points in this passage stand out?" Either ask students to work it out individually or designate a chorus and soloists to work together.

Language Arts

1. Assign an expressive line of dialog to each main character in the work you are reading. For example, Wilbur in *Charlotte's Web* might say, "Gee, won't somebody be my friend!" Then pick a student to sing or say each character's line every time the character is mentioned in the reading.

2. Assign students to create a song or jingle using a popular tune about a character or setting. Following is an example:

   Charlotte, Charlotte
   Spun a nice web.
   She copied down words
   To save Wilbur's head!

Make sure students get a chance to perform!

Math

Make up jingles to remember math facts or to memorize multiplication tables. Following is an example.

6 octopi can fish real great,
Eight arms each catch 48!
6 times 8 is . . . 48!

Social Studies

1. List five important facts you want students to remember. In pairs or groups have them create jingles or rhymes to make the information easy to remember. Give them such examples as, "In 1492, Columbus sailed the ocean blue," to get them started.

2. Assign students an easy tune (such as a nursery rhyme) to write a song about a famous person or place you are studying.

Strategy 2

Background Music

In Brief

Students start by matching well-known tunes with their emotional associations, and then learn to do the same exercise with classical music. Once their collection of background music is well established, they will use their music lists to choose background music for reading, visual, or role-play lessons.

Objectives

To increase comprehension and attention span

To encourage students to think about deep layers of emotion and meaning in their learning material by asking them to select the best background music for it

Background

By getting in touch with the emotions associated with particular musical selections, students will have easy access to a musical repertoire reflecting feelings and emotions to help explain and understand any subject matter.

Materials

one copy for each student of Library of Songs and Feelings work sheet (will be used in all lessons)

Lesson 1: My Music Library

Time

20 minutes (includes 5 minutes prep time)

Materials

old music books or song books (optional)

Preparation

Make copies of Library of Songs and Feelings work sheet.

Focus

Ask students, "What is it like to watch a scary movie on television when the sound is turned off? What about a sad movie? A funny movie?" Then ask them, "What is it that you lose?" Students will respond in a variety of ways. Some might say they miss the voices, the sound effects, the music (this response is the main one you're looking for). Some will say they notice that the movie is much less scary, funny, or sad.

Ask student volunteers to hum scary, sad, or funny music. Explain that motion picture and television directors often keep tapes, lists, and scores of various kinds of music so when they need the perfect background music for a certain kind of scene, they have a whole library of sounds to look through.

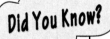

Did You Know? The part of the brain associated with music is also the part associated most with emotion? It's true . . . music soothes the savage beast!

Teach

Step 1: Tell students that as a class and as individuals you would like to begin keeping lists of potential background music and that today you will begin with simple, easily recognizable tunes.

Step 2: Pass out copies of Library of Songs and Feelings work sheet.

Step 3: Hum a few of the songs—remember, ham it up!—and have students identify the feelings (not the words) associated with the song. Ask them, "Can the feelings change if the song is sung faster or slower?"

Step 4: Work as a class to find tunes not on the list that evoke each feeling. Encourage students to think about it after the lesson is over, listen to music at home, and add songs to the list.

Lesson 2: Music is the Medium (optional)

Time

40 minutes (includes 10 to 20 minutes prep time)

Materials

a CD or tape player (humming selections from the song library can be sufficient to incorporate the background music strategy into lessons)

eight to ten tapes of a wide variety of classical (featuring different instruments and time periods) and contemporary (jazz, blues, African, instrumental rock and roll) music

markers or crayons and drawing paper

Focus

Ask students to recall a time when music affected their emotions; pick one or two students to share their experiences. Tell students the part of their brains that processes music also processes emotion, which is why music can sometimes make us smile or send tingles up our spines, or cause us to feel scared or sad. Use the two-fisted brain model from strategy 8 in chapter 1 to remind students where in their brains the limbic system is.

Teach

Step 1: Ask students to fold their sheets of drawing paper in half three times to create eight boxes (or fold two sheets of paper in half twice to create four boxes each).

Step 2: Explain that each box is for students to write and draw images, colors, and words that they think of after hearing a piece of music. Ask students not to draw anything in the boxes until after you have turned the music off and paused for a few seconds.

Step 3: Play your first selection for one to three minutes. Let students listen quietly.

Step 4: Turn off the music. Pause for a few seconds. Then ask students to write down images, colors, and words that they thought of when they heard that music.

Step 5: Finish all eight boxes using a variety of musical selections.

Step 6: Read off the titles of the selections when you finish so students can copy the names on their Library of Songs and Feelings work sheet under the appropriate headings.

Name: _____

Sad or Pensive
"Swing Low, Sweet Chariot"
"My Darlin' Clementine"
"Edelweiss"
"Kumbaya"
Other _____

Rejoicing or Resolved
"The Sound of Music"
"We Wish You a Merry Christmas"
"Under the Sea" (from Disney's *The Little Mermaid*)
Other _____

Brave or Strong
"Oklahoma!"
"You're a Grand Ole Flag"
"My Country 'Tis of Thee"
Other _____

Mad or Annoyed
"There's a Hole in the Bucket"
"R-E-S-P-E-C-T"
"Ain't Nothin' but a Hound Dog"
Other _____

Happy
"Zip-a-Dee-Doo-Dah"
"Small World"
"If You're Happy and You Know It"
"Day-O"
Other _____

Fearful or Scary
"Lions and Tiger and Bears, Oh My!"
Theme from *Jaws*
Other _____

Hurried
"Supercalifragilistic"
"Follow the Yellow Brick Road"
Other _____

Relaxed
"De Colores"
"Itsy Bitsy Spider"
Other _____

Lesson 3: Movie Music

Time

40 minutes (includes 5 minutes prep time)

Materials

Movie Synopsis handout

CD or tape player (optional for this activity)

Preparation

Make one copy of the Movie Synopsis handout and cut it along the scissors-lines to make seven cue cards.

Focus

Remind students that movie and television directors keep libraries of music to choose music for particular scenes. Tell students the time has come for them to direct their own movies. Hum a proud song such as "Grand Ole Flag" or the "Charge!" tune to show how excited you are!

Teach

Step 1: Ask students to review their Library of Songs and Feelings work sheet.

Step 2: Organize the students into groups of four or five, and give each group one Movie Synopsis cue card.

Step 3: Each group chooses a dramatic reader and the rest of the group plays the background music. Ask them to pick background music from their libraries that they think is most appropriate for their assigned movie synopses. Have the reader practice reading while the group performs the music.

Step 4: Have each group perform. Give Grammy Awards afterward!

Reflect

Ask students to discuss as a class and write in their thought journals how they think using background music helps them understand the material better.

Follow-up and Extension

Have students pick background music to hum while cleaning up, preparing to leave for the day, coming in from recess, and so on. Or, if you have a CD or tape player, play particular musical selections for certain types of activities (Handel's *Water Music* or Vivaldi's *The Four Seasons* for math and cooperative learning or silent reading; Tchaikovsky's *Marche Slav* or *Chariots of Fire* sound track for cleanup and physical education warm-ups; and so on).

Cut along lines, and give one synopsis to each group.

The monster lurks in the passage. It wants to destroy everything in its path. The hero feels tingles up her spine. She knows something is wrong in this place; something doesn't quite make sense. She has brought her flashlight and uses it to look around. She must find the answers to the puzzle. Will she make it out alive?

Puppy dog Henry has finally found a home. He jumps from one master to another. A small child squeals with delight at the puppy's playful nibbling. They love him! They want to keep him! No more eating out of garbage cans. No more dog fights in the alley down the street. From now on he has a warm hearth and a pillow for his head.

Why did that mean bully take Sara's skateboard? He kicked it right out from under her feet while she was still skating. Sara's scratched knees hurt and she felt her face get hot. She was going to get that board back, and she wasn't going to get help from anyone. This time she'd had enough. This time she was going to take care of that bully of the neighborhood. This time that bully would not be laughing!

The explorer used her strong hand to brush back the sweat and grime from her eyes. They were finally at the top of the mountain. The wind blew hard as she climbed to the precipice to look down. Before her was a new ocean, a great land, all that she had hoped for! Her heart pounded and she could hear the cheers rising from the workers as they each reached the edge of the mountain and saw the miracle for themselves. Land and ocean, as far as the eye could see!

Jim squeezed his eyes shut and tried not to let the tears escape. They had left him behind! All that planning and organizing with his friends, and when the day for the big trip was finally here, his friends got in the car and left without him. He was only minutes late! Couldn't they have waited just a little longer? He had worked so hard to earn the money for the tent and supplies. They had all worked so hard convincing their parents and mowing lawns for money. Now he was left behind!

Oh, no! Michael looked at his watch; was it possible? He was just waking up and he had only fifteen minutes to get to school! The big math test was scheduled first thing in the morning! He leapt out of bed and ran for his clothes. He grabbed a few things out of his drawers and headed for the bathroom to brush his teeth and throw some water on his face while he dressed. Running out the door he grabbed his book bag and a cold Pop Tart. Five minutes left; could he make it?

The class broke into a cheer! The news had finally come back; they were chosen as the winners of the school contest. They had worked hard to involve every neighborhood in an emergency preparedness plan. Knocking on door after door, asking for block leaders, and getting signatures was not easy. It was hard work! But they had won the school contest and it was worth it! They felt good about their accomplishment. They also felt good about the reward! Ice cream sundaes and an extra field trip of their choice!

Multilple Intelligences Made Easy © 1999 Zephyr Press, Inc., Tucson, Arizona

Applying the Strategy to Curriculum

Any dramatic passage from a social studies, language arts, or science text will benefit from a little background music. Ask student volunteers to hum a selection from their Library of Songs and Feelings while another student reads the passage aloud.

Did You Know?

Music used in conjunction with a lesson can teach 60 percent of the content in 5 percent of the time of lessons taught without music (Jensen 1994a).

Strategy 3

Word Symphonies

In Brief

Students learn the meanings of six musical notations, practice the techniques with a well-known song, then apply the same notation system to written materials in order to emphasize important parts of the readings.

Objective

To give students practice in prioritizing and organizing information by asking them to use musical notation marks as emphasis codes

Background

Musical notation is the language of music. Musicians understand that a *crescendo* means to play progressively louder and a *decrescendo* means to play progressively softer. They know that a *slur* means to run notes into each other stretching . . . out . . . the . . . notes, while a *staccato* means to make brief, separated jabs at the notes. The word *allegro* means to go fast, while *adagio* means to go slow. These notations can be enjoyable and helpful when used as a way to bring deeper expression and emphasis to learning materials.

Lesson 1: Musical Emphasis

Time

30 minutes (includes 5 minutes prep time)

Materials

large index cards (optional)

a familiar and popular song ("This Old Man," "Yankee Doodle," and so on)

Preparation

Write the symbols for *crescendo, decrescendo, slur, staccato* and the words *allegro* and *adagio* on the chalkboard or copy them onto an overhead.

Focus

Ask students, "How many different ways can a word be said?" Ask for student volunteers to try to sing the word

Supercalifragilisticexpealidocious

several times, each in a different way from the last. List the ways they are singing the word on the chalkboard: loud, soft, silly, low, high, short, long, and so on. Compliment them on the wide variety of sounds they created. Explain that in music there are special symbols that tell musicians how to play notes in different ways.

Teach

Step 1: Tell students they are going to learn four symbols and two words.

Step 2: Draw the symbols for *crescendo* and *decrescendo* on the board. Explain that these symbols tell musicians to get gradually louder and gradually softer.

Step 3: Sing one line of the song that you have chosen to practice, demonstrating what the crescendo and decrescendo sound like.

Step 4: Tell students you are going to sing the song together, but this time you are going to hold your arms in the shape of the crescendo and decrescendo so the students can practice getting gradually louder and gradually softer. Make sure you hold your arms so that they look like a crescendo or decrescendo sign from the students' point of view, not your own. You may choose to draw the symbols on the chalkboard and point to each instead.

Step 5: Once the students are comfortable with crescendo and decrescendo, draw the *staccato* symbol on the board. Explain that it looks like a period and goes either under or above the note. It tells musicians to play the note sharply and briefly, like a jab. Sing the first line of the song you have chosen with staccato notes. Let the students try it.

Step 6: Start the line without staccato and then point to the staccato on the board and change to staccato notes halfway through.

Step 7: Explain the *slur*, an arc that connects two notes. It means the notes should run together (like slurring your words). Sing a line of the practice song with slurs.

Step 8: Write the first line of your song on the board, putting staccato symbols above some syllables and words, and slur symbols between others. Let students come up and practice singing the way you have written the line. Following is an example.

I've been working on the railroad, all my live long days.

Step 9: Introduce *allegro* and *adagio.* Explain that *allegro* written above the music means to play the music quickly, and *adagio* means to play it slowly. Practice your song using both allegro and adagio, then a combination of both.

Step 10: To solidify student understanding, practice the six notations with your song. To signal when to change, flash note cards, point to symbols on the board, or make up hand signals for each notation.

Lesson 2: Saying It with Emphasis

Time

25 minutes (includes 5 minutes prep time)

Materials

one copy for each student of Practice Passages work sheet

large index cards (optional)

Preparation

Write the symbols for *crescendo, decrescendo, slur,* and *staccato* on the board or on an overhead. Write *allegro* and *adagio* on the chalkboard or on an overhead. Make copies of the Practice Passages work sheet.

Focus

Review the musical notation symbols and terms: *staccato, slur, crescendo, decrescendo, adagio,* and *allegro.* Ask students how they think the same notations could be used with written material. Discuss and accept any answer or explanation.

Teach

Step 1: Tell students they are going to use the symbols to highlight passages of reading material.

Step 2: Choose three students to read aloud each of the three passages on the work sheet in a normal voice.

Step 3: Ask students to look carefully at the first passage. Ask them, "If you wanted to make this passage more exciting to listen to or easier to understand, which part would you say gradually louder or softer? Which symbol should we put in to show that change?" You want students to recognize that as the climax grows closer, or as the information gets more important, the reading should grow louder.

Step 4: Ask them, "Which part could be clearer with staccato? Maybe the details?"

Step 5: Ask them, "Which part might be nicer with slurs? Maybe a dreamy part?"

Step 6: Ask them, "Which part should get faster or slower?"

Step 7: Divide the class into groups of four or five and ask the groups to answer the same questions about the next two passages. Make sure they understand that they don't have to use every symbol in every passage.

Step 8: After ten minutes, have each group perform its passage.

Reflect

Ask students, "How do the musical notations help us to better understand what we are reading?" Through discussion, encourage the class to understand that the notation highlights important parts of the reading and helps their ears hear the details.

Follow-up and Extension

Use the musical notations as part of a reading comprehension test. Ask students to highlight the climax of a story with crescendo marks or indicate important details with staccato symbols.

Applying the Strategy to Curriculum

To test comprehension of any passage from a social studies, language arts, or science textbook, have students copy a sentence or paragraph and use musical notation to highlight and express. Don't forget to let them perform their readings.

Science

Use crescendo and decrescendo to show where the most important part of a scientific experiment happens. Use staccato to pick out important details to remember. Students can make cards for each of the symbols and hold them up during class readings. Or make photocopies of the reading material for students to mark up with musical notation.

Language Arts

1. Make copies of part of the current reading, and have students add musical notation to cue themselves when reading aloud.
2. Have students use musical notation to mark class speeches or presentations so they will read with expression.
3. Have student use musical notation in a poetry recital.
4. Have students make and hold up musical notation cards to show when they think a passage is covering an important detail or an important main idea.

Math

1. As a class, compare crescendo and decrescendo to the *greater than* and *less than* symbols using a Venn diagram. Ask them, "How are they alike? How are they different?"
2. Bring copies of a musical score into class and have students count each occurrence of each notation symbol. Have them chart the numbers on a bar graph. Ask, "Is one kind used more often than others?" Do comparative graphs with various kinds of music.

Strategy 3 Work Sheet

Practice Passages

Name: _____

Mark each passage using the musical notations for crescendo, decrescendo, staccato, and slur, and the words *allegro* and *adagio*. Then read the passages aloud using the notations as guides.

PASSAGE 1 (whole class)

The student squirmed in his seat. He had forgot about the math test. He had not practiced his multiplication tables or long division. He had played video games instead. Now he was stuck. He was sure to fail the test. He raised his hand to ask if he could go to the rest room. All the other students in the room had their hands up, too. Everyone wanted to go to the rest room. The teacher shook his head and began to pass out the tests. The student groaned and sank in his seat. Oh, why hadn't he studied? How could he have forgot? He felt as though he were going to be sick. His hand shook as he took the paper, and when he finally looked at it, he gasped. He knew all the answers! The test was easy; it was all stuff he could do. He smiled. He was going to ace this test!

PASSAGE 2 (small groups or independently)

The rope was long. It reached high up to the ceiling of the gym. Karen's assignment was to climb the rope to the top. Every six feet or so the rope had a knot to grab onto. Karen began her climb up . . . up . . . up the rope. Her classmates watched from below. She reached the first knot, then the second, then the third . . . She kept up her strength to the fourth knot but had to strain to reach the fifth and sixth until, finally, she touched the top. She could hear her friends down below clapping, and she felt thrilled. She held on tight and came down the rope fast!

PASSAGE 3 (small groups or independently)

The human brain has many important parts. The *cerebellum,* located at the bottom and to the back of the brain, controls much of the motor coordination and movement of the body. In the middle of the brain is a part called the *thalamus,* which receives messages about pain and temperature from the nervous system and sends those messages to the upper part of the brain. The upper cap of the brain is the *cerebrum.* It is where people do all their thinking, planning, and remembering. The covering of the cerebrum is wrinkled so that more brain can fit into a smaller space . . . many animals have smooth cerebrums. Finally, the *medulla* is located at the back of the neck at the top of the spinal cord. It is the most crucial part of the brain because it is the part that keeps the heart beating and the lungs breathing.

Multiple Intelligences Made Easy © 1999 Zephyr Press, Inc., Tucson, Arizona

Social Studies

Have students mark a time line from a historical period with musical notation. Following is an example of questions and answers regarding a writing on the Revolution.

- When does it begin to crescendo? (During the Boston Tea Party and the massacre)
- When might you hear allegro? (When the minutemen are getting ready and Paul Revere is riding to warn the colonials)

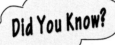

More than one hundred descendants of Johann Sebastian Bach have been cathedral organists (Louis 1983).

Strategy 4

Math Music

In Brief

Students learn to count beats and work out rhythmic patterns using the whole note, the half note, the quarter note, the eighth note, and the sixteenth note. They transform the rhythms they learn into simple math problems of fraction addition.

Objective

To use rhythm and musical notes as math manipulatives

Background

Rhythm and musical notes are naturally designed to be used with math. Even the terminology of music suits math. Quarter notes and half notes are fractions of whole notes. In music we "count" the beat and use "measures." This strategy takes advantage of those similarities to bring music to math and to bring students to math through music.

Lesson 1: Quarter Notes

Time

20 to 22 minutes (includes 5 to 7 minutes prep time)

Materials

one copy for each student of Rhythms work sheet

Preparation

Make copies of Rhythms work sheet. Copy three rhythm lines on the chalkboard.

Focus

Tap out a simple rhythm by clapping 1, 2, 3, 4. Ask students to copy your rhythm. Try a few, more complex rhythms: 1, 2, wait, wait, 3, 4, wait, wait; 1, 2, 3, wait, 1, 2, 3, wait. Ask students, "How might these rhythms be similar to math?" Discuss and accept any answers or suggestions.

Teach

Step 1. Tell students that in its most basic form, music is really about counting beats and playing on some beats and not on others.

Step 2: Copy the first rhythm pattern example onto the board. Have students count evenly with the numbers and clap on each number where they see a bell. Ask if any students know how to continue the pattern in writing or by clapping. Then try the next two patterns.

Step 3: Explain that each group of numbers separated by a vertical line is called a *measure* in music. In the examples we are using, there are four counts in each measure.

Step 4: Let them use the Rhythms work sheet on page 62 to make up their own rhythms and patterns, either in groups, alone in class, or as homework.

REMINDER

Lesson 1 can be an ongoing enjoyable activity to help your students develop rhythm, and patterning and counting skills.
The more comfortable they are with this lesson, the easier lesson 2 will become.

Lesson 2: Whole and Half Notes

Time

40 to 42 minutes (includes 5 to 7 minutes prep time)

Materials

three 5-by-7-inch index cards

one copy for each student of Musical Fractions 1 work sheet

Preparation

Make copies of Musical Fractions 1 work sheet. Draw a quarter note, a half note, and a whole note, each on a separate large index card.

   ♩ = 1 beat   ♩ = 2 beats   ○ = 4 beats
  quarter note   half note   whole note

Focus

Write the following blank rhythm line on the chalkboard:

1 2 3 4 / 1 2 3 4 / 1 2 3 4 / 1 2 3 4

Strategy 4 Work Sheet

Rhythms

Name: _____

1 2 3 4 | 1 2 3 4 | 1 2 3 4 | 1 2 3 4 | 1 2 3 4 | 1 2 3 4

1 2 3 4 | 1 2 3 4 | 1 2 3 4 | 1 2 3 4 | 1 2 3 4 | 1 2 3 4

1 2 3 4 | 1 2 3 4 | 1 2 3 4 | 1 2 3 4 | 1 2 3 4 | 1 2 3 4

1 2 3 4 | 1 2 3 4 | 1 2 3 4 | 1 2 3 4 | 1 2 3 4 | 1 2 3 4

1 2 3 4 | 1 2 3 4 | 1 2 3 4 | 1 2 3 4 | 1 2 3 4 | 1 2 3 4

1 2 3 4 | 1 2 3 4 | 1 2 3 4 | 1 2 3 4 | 1 2 3 4 | 1 2 3 4

1 2 3 4 | 1 2 3 4 | 1 2 3 4 | 1 2 3 4 | 1 2 3 4 | 1 2 3 4

Multliple Intelligences Made Easy © 1999 Zephyr Press, Inc., Tucson, Arizona

Have a student come up and write a rhythm. Perform the rhythm as a class. Ask students how they would make the sound if two of the claps were connected. Some students will suggest clapping twice, but explain that you want the notes to actually run into each other, to slur together and become one longer note. Teach them to hum it or to sing la-aa, la-aa.

Teach

Step 1: Show students the quarter-note card. Explain that a quarter note lasts exactly one beat, just like the ones the class used in the previous lesson to invent rhythms. Clap four quarter notes. (See the following example.)

Step 2: Show them the half-note card. Explain that a half note lasts for half of the measure. It is twice as long as a quarter note. Compare them by singing la, la-aa. (See the following example.)

Step 3: Show students the whole-note card. Explain that a whole note is held for the whole measure and can be sung la-aa-aa-aa. (See the following example.)

Step 4: Hand out copies of Musical Fractions 1 work sheet and let students invent their own rhythms. Remind them to use all three kinds of notes.

Step 5: After twenty minutes, ask for student volunteers to perform their favorite new rhythm.

Step 6: Tell students they are going to translate some musical rhythms into fractions. Copy the following example onto the chalkboard, show students how the notes translate into fractions, and explain that they can add the fractions to equal the number of measures in the rhythm.

♩ ♩ ♩ ♩ |
1 2 3 4
La La La La

$\frac{1}{4} + \frac{1}{4} + \frac{1}{4} + \frac{1}{4} = \frac{4}{4} = 1$ (measure)

♩ ♩
1 2 3 4
La-aa La-aa

$\frac{1}{2} + \frac{1}{2} = \frac{2}{2} = 1$ (measure)

Step 7: Copy the following musical math problems onto the chalkboard and solve them as a class. Then let students work alone or in pairs to complete Musical Fractions 1 work sheet.

♩ ♩ | ♩ ♩
1 2 3 4 | 1 2 3 4
La-aa La-aa La-aa La-aa

$\frac{1}{2} + \frac{1}{2} + \frac{1}{2} + \frac{1}{2} = \frac{4}{2} = 2$ (measures)

♩ ♩ ♩ |
1 2 3 4
La La La-aa

$\frac{1}{4} + \frac{1}{4} + \frac{1}{2} = \frac{4}{4} = 1$ (measure)

Reflect

Ask students, "How are music and fractions alike?" Discuss students' answers as a class.

Strategy 4 Work Sheet

Name: _____

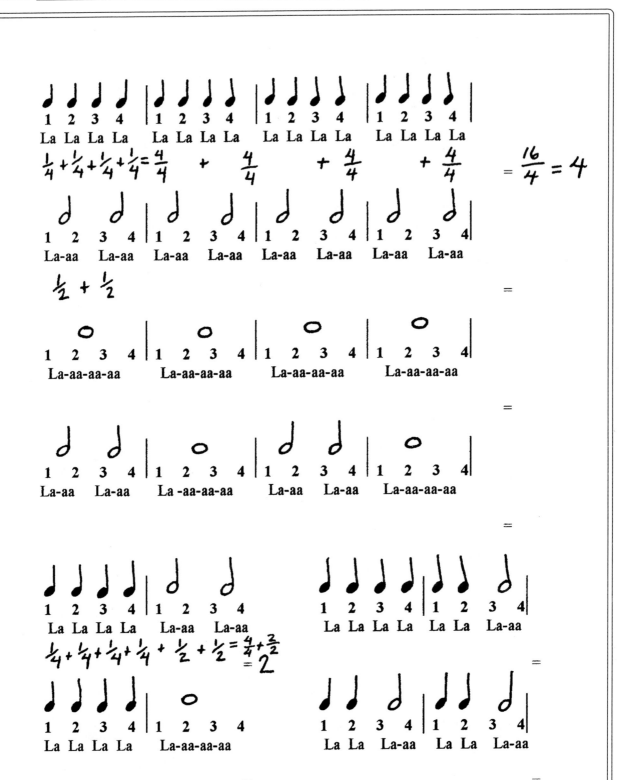

Lesson 3: More Quickly Now

Time

30 to 32 minutes (includes 5 to 7 minutes prep time)

Materials

5-by-7-inch index cards

one copy for each student of Rhythms work sheet

one copy for each student of Musical Fractions 2 work sheet

Preparation

Make copies of Rhythm work sheet and Musical Fractions 2 work sheet. On the large index cards, draw the following notes:

♪ = 1/2 beat
eighth note   ♬ = 1/4 beat or 2 ♫
sixteenth note

Focus

Write a blank rhythm line on the chalkboard:

1 2 3 4 / 1 2 3 4 / 1 2 3 4 / 1 2 3 4

Have a student come up and write a rhythm, using a combination of quarter, half, and whole notes. Perform the rhythm as a class.

Teach

Step 1: Show them the eighth-note card. Explain that an eighth note lasts exactly one half of a quarter-note clap, so there are two eighth notes in one beat, and eight eighth notes in one measure. Clap twice, twice as fast as for a quarter note, in order for two eighth notes to equal one quarter note. Clap this fast eight times for eight eighth notes, which equals four quarter notes, which equals one measure. (See the following example.)

| 1 | 2 | 3 | 4 |
| clap, clap | clap, clap | clap, clap | clap, clap |

Step 2: Show students the sixteenth-note card. Explain that the sixteenth note is one-fourth of a beat, meaning that four claps have to happen in the space of one quarter-note clap. There are sixteen sixteenth notes in a measure. Sing or clap. (See the following example.)

LaLaLaLa, LaLaLaLa, LaLaLaLa, LaLaLaLa

Step 3: Hand out blank Rhythm work sheets and let students make up their own rhythms using both eighth and sixteenth notes.

Step 4: After fifteen minutes, ask volunteers to perform one of the rhythms they came up with.

Step 5: Tell students they are going to translate more musical rhythms into fractions. (See the following example.)

$$\frac{2}{8} + \frac{2}{8} + \frac{2}{8} + \frac{2}{8} = \frac{8}{8} \qquad = 1 \text{ (measure)}$$

$$\frac{4}{16} + \frac{4}{16} + \frac{4}{16} + \frac{4}{16} = \frac{16}{16} \qquad = 1 \text{(measure)}$$

Step 6: Write the following examples on the chalkboard and solve them as a class. Then let students work alone or in pairs to do the Musical Fractions 2 work sheet on page 68.

Name: _____

1 2 3 4 | 1 2 3 4 | 1 2 3 4 | 1 2 3 4

$\frac{2}{8} + \frac{2}{8} + \frac{2}{8} + \frac{2}{8} + \frac{4}{16} + \frac{4}{16} + \frac{4}{16} + \frac{4}{16} + \frac{2}{8} + \frac{2}{8} + \frac{2}{8} + \frac{2}{8} + \frac{4}{16} + \frac{4}{16} + \frac{4}{16} + \frac{4}{16} = \frac{16}{8} + \frac{32}{16} = 4$

1 2 3 4 | 1 2 3 4 | 1 2 3 4 | 1 2 3 4

=

1 2 3 4 | 1 2 3 4 | 1 2 3 4 | 1 2 3 4

=

1 2 3 4 | 1 2 3 4 | 1 2 3 4 | 1 2 3 4

=

Now write your own!

1 2 3 4 | 1 2 3 4   1 2 3 4 | 1 2 3 4

=   =

1 2 3 4 | 1 2 3 4   1 2 3 4 | 1 2 3 4

=   =

Multiple Intelligences Made Easy © 1999 Zephyr Press, Inc., Tucson, Arizona

Reflect

Ask students, "How are eighth and sixteenth notes different from whole and half notes? Which has more parts? Which is bigger? How are musical notes similar to fractions?"

Follow-up and Extension

As a class, complete a Venn diagram comparing and contrasting math with music.

Strategy 5

Musical Analogies

In Brief

Students make up rhythms to describe certain body actions, moods, and places. Then they compare various kinds of music with places, time periods, shapes, colors, and people.

Objective

To compare and contrast music and rhythm with subject matter to understand more deeply and widely the subject matter

Background

Analogies develop broad perspectives by helping students think beyond what is written on the page. When asked to complete the analogy "Body systems are like community systems because . . . " students are suddenly exposed to a deeper level of thinking about the human body. They begin to understand how the systems interact and depend on one another in the same way that a city's infrastructure interacts. You can have students create similar analogies with music by asking such questions as, "Can you create a rhythm that is like the march of the Redcoats in the Revolutionary War?" or "How is the tune of 'Oh My Darlin' Clementine' similar to a coal mine?"

Lesson 1: Where Does the Music Live?

Time

35 to 45 minutes (includes 10 to 20 minutes prep time)

Materials

thought journals

photographs or pictures of various kinds of famous places and people

CD or tape player and a variety of CDs or tapes (optional but preferable; without these you must hum or tap)

Focus

Tap out a fast rhythm and then a slow rhythm. Ask students, "Which rhythm is more like a subway train? Which is more like a horse and carriage? Why?" Tap out a complex rhythm, then a simple one: bum de-ditta-de-ditta bum de-ditta bum, bum de-ditta-de-ditta bum de-ditta bum"; "bum-bum-bum-bum-de, bum-bum-bum-bum-de." Ask students, "Which is more like Eeyore and which is more like Tigger. Why?"

Teach

Step 1: Tell students that music has always been used to describe feelings, places, people, and events. Because music goes right to the heart of our emotions, it is sometimes better at reflecting emotions than words.

Step 2: Tape up or hold up two pictures of two very different places from books or posters, such as the Taj Mahal and a log cabin. Tell students to study the places while they listen to a piece of music.

Step 3: Play a music selection on the player or hum a tune.

Step 4: Ask students which place is more like the song and why. Accept any answers, but encourage discussion.

Step 5: Take the posters down. Play or hum a new tune for a few minutes. Ask students to work in groups of four or five to describe a place that goes with the music. Have each group pick a reporter to share with the class the group's description.

Step 6: Repeat steps 2 through 5 to compare a sport or physical motion to music, to compare various moods to music, to compare colors and shapes to music, or to compare famous people to music.

Reflect

Ask students to write about the following question in their thought journals: "How does comparing a place or time period or person to a piece of music help you better understand that place, time period, or person?"

Lesson 2: Match that Tune

Time

20 minutes

Materials

social studies or language arts learning textbooks

rhythm instruments (optional)

Focus

Tap out a fast rhythm, then a slow rhythm. Ask students, "Which is more like a dinosaur? Which is more like a bird? Why?"

Teach

Step 1: Tell students that African peoples and some American Indian tribes have long used drums and rhythms to communicate news or tell a story.

Step 2: Divide the class into groups of three or four. Assign each group to come up with rhythms to represent the main characters in the current readings or the places or event in their history studies.

Step 3: After ten minutes have each group perform its rhythms while the rest of the class tries to guess which rhythm goes with each character, place, or event (write the possibilities on the board).

Reflect

Ask students to discuss their answers to the following questions: "What would be better about communicating with drums and rhythms than with words? What would be worse?"

Follow-up and Extension

Ask students, "How is 'Taps' like the end of a day? Can you make a tune like recess time?" As a class, ask students to make up rhythms or sounds to signify recess, time to go home, and job well done.

Applying the Strategy to Curriculum

Pick out something you are presently studying: a period in history, a famous person, a character in a book, and so on. Play two different pieces of music and ask students to explain which selection is most like that time period, person, or character. Visual aids—a poster or picture of the person, place, or event—can help catalyze their thought processes.

Science

1. Learn Morse code. Then have students invent their own sound code.

2. Research the part of the human brain that deals with music and emotion. Ask students to hypothesize why music gives us such a sense of feeling and story.

Language Arts

1. Take any reading passage, then choose setting or character as the topic. Let students invent rhythms or select music that is like the character or setting.

2. Hum a tune after reading the beginning of a story. Ask how that tune is like or unlike the story.

3. Play two pieces of classical music. Have students listen and decide which is most like their reading selection.

4. Play a musical selection or tap out a rhythm. Then have a student read something from her journal, a report, or some other assignment. Have the class explain how the musical selection is like or unlike the writing sample.

Social Studies

1. Learn historical songs. Ask how the music is like or unlike the particular time period or event.

2. Invent rhythms or melodies that are like various important events, people, armies, and so on.

3. Show a historical picture. Play two pieces of music. Ask how each is like the music.

Strategy 6

Composing a Song

In Brief

Students critique how well a particular melody matches the opinion put forth by the lyrics of a song, then they choose a melody with which to write a song expressing their own opinions about a particular issue.

Objective

To enhance students' abilities to retell a story or argue a point of view through the composition of an original song

Background

Music is a powerful communicator because it not only involves words, but also tugs directly at our emotions through the melody. Students who have enjoyed learning about and using the various musical elements covered in this chapter will enjoy taking on the challenge of converting what they learned into music.

Lesson 1: Singing a Story

Time

30 minutes (includes 10 minutes prep time)

Materials

CD or tape player

a selection of two to five songs that tell a story, express an opinion, and so on (examples: "Cat's in the Cradle" by Harry Chapin, "Where Do the Children Play" by Cat Stevens, "Wind Beneath My Wings" by Bette Midler, "Don't Worry, Be Happy" by Bobby McFerrin)

Preparation

Gather recordings of two to five songs.

Focus

Ask students, "What are some of the elements that make a song interesting? Do the stories or words of a song usually match the sound of the music?" Discuss and accept any answers.

Teach

Step 1: Tell students that soon they will be writing their own songs and you want them to be aware of how melody affects the mood of what is being sung.

Step 2: Play one of the musical selections.

Step 3: Ask students to paraphrase what is being said in the music.

Step 4: Ask students their opinion of how well the sound of the music matches the words being sung.

Step 5: Repeat steps 1 through 3 with the other music selections.

Lesson 2: Write a Song

Time

35 minutes, 30 to 60 minutes during the next school week

Materials

thought journals

popular songbooks (optional, but helpful)

Focus

Ask a student to summarize "Three Little Pigs." Ask another student what melody would express the feelings and experiences of the pigs. What about the wolf?

Teach

Step 1: Ask students to pick a fairy tale villain or supporting character (Grandma in "Little Red Riding Hood," the prince or a dwarf in "Snow White," and so on).

Step 2: Tell students to think of a song that has music that matches the feelings and experiences of the characters they selected. Have them write new words for the music that retells the story as if that character were singing the song. Students can do this project individually or in groups of two or three.

Step 3: Give students a significant amount of time. Consider providing a half hour of class time, plus small group work time and homework time over one to two weeks. Students can write drafts and share them with partners or with you for feedback.

Step 4: Once students have finished their songs, give them a chance to perform—and don't forget the Grammy Awards!

Reflect

Ask students to write in their thought journals about the differences between telling a story with music rather than with words alone.

Follow-up and Extension

Offer song writing as an alternative to report writing or speech making.

Applying Strategy

Science

Have students compose a song about a famous inventor or scientist.

Language Arts

1. Reteach lesson 2 using a supporting character or antagonist from the current reading. Ask individual students or small groups to pick appropriate music and rewrite the song as if the character were retelling the story or a part of the story.

> Students will want to perform their compositions. Dim the lights, use flashlights for spotlights, and make it a real performance!
>
> **REMINDER**

2. Use this strategy at the end of a story line or when a character has just had an emotional experience that can be told in a song. Give students time to complete the project; you might even have them do it as homework.
3. Have students rewrite their own stories or poems as songs.
4. Challenge highly musical students to write their own music.
5. As a class, write a song about an activity you do together. Pick out music together, write the song together, learn it and perform it together. (Make it a song about eating lunch at school!)

Social Studies

1. Have students tell a famous person's story through a song.
2. Make up a person who sings a song about a particular event (a Redcoat singing about the battle against the minutemen, a wife singing about her husband the gold miner, a member of the Iroquois Confederacy singing about the Pilgrims, and so on).

3

Bodily-Kinesthetic Intelligence

Remember the old adage, once you learn to ride a bike, you never forget? Well, it's true, and children ache to get up out of their seats and learn by doing! Physical learning—by playing a game, learning a skill, acting out, or moving around—allows the body's memory to help the brain learn and remember, and it can be enjoyable and relieve stress, as well.

> Learning through movement will probably be completely foreign to many of your students. As you teach the lessons in this chapter, preview each one by summarizing the activities and goals for your students.

REMINDER

Athletes, actors, choreographers, construction workers, and inventors use bodily-kinesthetic intelligence to develop coordination and physical expression for sports, entertainment, art, or to refine a conceptual idea. Any teacher willing to act it out and ham it up will find it easy to use the strategies in this chapter to incorporate physical learning into his curriculum. Along with the ideas presented here, look for other ways to add body smarts to the regular curriculum. Try teaching folk and cultural dances in social studies and language arts. Make up new games that imitate scientific processes, such as a version of tag that imitates natural selection or a ball toss that shows how cells send information. Use sign language and physical gestures to communicate. And don't forget your standard physical education curriculum. Children need to get outside and move their bodies now more than ever.

Did You Know?

○ On average, children watch television fifteen hours per week. This time coupled with time spent sitting at a school desk leaves little room for physical fitness in a child's life.

Strategy 1

Easy Role-Play

In Brief

In lesson 1, students learn to transform nonfiction and fiction reading passages into dialog and speeches. In lesson 2, they experiment with using different kinds of gestures to evoke certain ideas, emotions, or character traits. In lesson 3, the class learns to make quick and easy props, then translates all three lessons into instant class performances.

Objective

To involve students in spontaneous acting scenes, ideas, and events in order to give them hands-on understanding

Background

Adults can often recall elementary school performances: plays in which they had only one line (which they forgot), holiday programs in which the whole class had to dress as green elves, and so on. These experiences stay with us because they are funny, but also because they involve our bodies, which ties them effectively to our memories. Many teachers get very excited when a play comes along that relates to a social studies topic. They know students will enjoy performing and that they will gain a tremendous learning experience to boot. The Easy Role-Play strategy does not replace those special performances, but it makes it easy to use performances in the classroom often and in spontaneous ways.

> **REMINDER**
>
> Students who have been contained in classroom seats overreact at their first chance on stage. Set up the Easy Role-Play carefully the first few times. Remind students about appropriate behavior and select actors with self-control at first. Depending on the needs of the class, you may want to hold a brief rehearsal with three or four students who can demonstrate the activity to the rest of the class.

Lesson 1: Dip into Dialogue

Time

15 minutes (including 5 minutes prep time)

Materials

current reading selections from either social studies or language arts

Preparation

Select a scene from a social studies or language arts reading that contains either dialogue or a detailed description of a situation from which creating dialogue would be relatively easy. Set the stage for the lesson by assigning students particular roles and describing the scene. If you can't find a good scene in the textbooks, consider a visit to the library to find a biography or historical narrative pertaining to your current unit of study.

Focus

Discuss with students how different people can say the same thing in a variety of ways. As an example, ask for three volunteers to announce that it is time for recess. Ask the first volunteer to pretend to be the principal; ask the second volunteer to pretend to be a student who loves to play basketball; ask the third volunteer to pretend to be the custodian in charge of the lawn and blacktop. Ask them "Why would each person say the same thing differently? What is each person thinking when he or she says it?"

Teach

Step 1: Tell students they are going to practice speaking as if they were other people.

Step 2: Ask students to open their texts to the scene you selected. If there is dialog, select students to play the parts (skip narration areas). If there is no dialog, create characters to play the events (for example, an Arawak watching boats filled with explorers land on her shore, a crew member rowing the boat to shore and hoping to find fruit so he won't get scurvy).

Step 3: Ask students either to think about how their characters would say the lines, or to make up a line or two that their characters would say. Remind them that the goal of the exercise is to read with the feelings and expression that the character would probably have in that situation. After they have selected and practiced saying their lines with expression, have them perform from their seats.

Step 4: Let the rest of the class critique the performance after reminding them that, during a critique, compliments always come first! Time permitting, think up additional lines and characters and perform again with a second set of students.

Reflect

Ask students what feels different about pretending to be a character as opposed to reading about a character. Ask the class the following questions: "Does pretending help you understand the character better? In what ways?" Remember to allow for differing points of view; some students may prefer just reading.

Lesson 2: Pick a Pose

Time

15 minutes (including 5 minutes prep time)

Materials

current reading selection from social studies or language arts

Preparation

Gather a list of the major and minor characters in the current reading.

Focus

Ask for volunteers to demonstrate answers to the following questions: "How would a principal stand or move her arms when telling you to stop running in the halls?" "How would a parent stand or move to tell you to stop running in the house?" "How would a younger sibling stand or move to ask you not to run over the sand castle she just finished building?" Discuss as a class the differences among the various gestures.

Teach

Step 1: Tell students they are going to practice making gestures as if they were other people.

Step 2: Ask students to open their texts to the scene you selected.

Step 3: If the text contains a description of a gesture or movement, choose students to demonstrate the gestures or movements. If not, assign characters in the selection to students and ask them to design postures or gestures that fit their respective characters.

Step 4: Have students perform their gestures and ask the class to critique. How believable were their body movements and facial expressions? Could the class guess who the student-actors were portraying? Consider having a small Academy Awards ceremony.

Step 5: Let other students try the same gestures or invent additional characters for the scene.

Reflect

Ask students in what ways pretending to be a character feels different from reading about a character. Does pretending make them understand the character more?

Lesson 3: Props Add Pizazz

Time

15 minutes (includes 5 minutes prep time)

Materials

current reading selections from social studies or language arts

Preparation

Select a reading in language arts or social studies that depicts one or more characters performing tasks, with or without props.

Focus

Ask for student volunteers to use a chair to show how a preschooler sits, or a teenager at a bus stop, a nervous person, a relaxed person, and so on. Let students use a pencil to pretend to be a writer, a reporter, a musician, a preschooler, and so on. Ask students, "How do props help us see and understand a character better?"

Teach

Step 1: Tell students they are going to use props as if they were other people.

Step 2: Ask students to open their text to the scene you selected.

Step 3: If there is a description of the use of props, pick students to find similar props in the classroom (a chair, a broom, a book, a ruler, a pencil, and so on). Ask them to use the props to show the movements, gestures, or attitudes of the characters.

Step 4: If there is no description of the use of a prop in the reading, pick two to five students to pretend to be characters in the reading or imagined characters who could have been in the situation. Ask them to select props to act out the gestures, movements, or poses that depict the invented characters.

Step 5: Let other students act out the same gestures or invent additional characters for the scene.

Reflect

Ask students in what ways pretending to be a character feels different from reading about a character. Does pretending help them understand the character better? Does using props help them understand the character better?

Follow-up and Extension

When a class or playground conflict arises, wait until tensions have been resolved, then offer the conflict as an easy role-play. Let students select and act out roles and ask them to design scenarios that help resolve the conflict peacefully.

Applying the Strategy to Curriculum

Science

Have students act out a discovery that is covered in your science unit.

Language Arts

1. Any dialog in any reading provides an opportunity to divide parts and have the students perform. They can perform just the words, or they can add gestures and props, depending on the time available and the setting where the dialog takes place.

2. When a character displays a particular attitude (annoyance, boredom, excitement, aloofness, and so on), stop the reading, grab a broom or chair, and have students perform the attitude. Or have the whole class make facial expressions to show how a character is feeling. This technique is also good to use with feeling vocabulary words: *enthusiastic, isolated, remorseful, fearful, bored,* and so on.

3. Jot down character names on index cards, hand them out to students, and let students come to the front of the class and ad-lib a performance of a scene you have just read.

4. Allow students to tell the story in skit form.

Math

Ask students to voice their opinions on a particular issue by making an expressive face. Then have them create a human bar graph by lining up people whose faces look alike.

Social Studies

1. Write down historical characters or events on index cards, and ask students to ad-lib lines, gestures, or actions using props.

2. Fold a newspaper into a hat, and ask students to wear it in various ways to portray various characters from a historical period.

3. Ask students to perform one-paragraph speeches from the point of view of characters who participated in the event (for example, the wife of a gold miner, child whose dad—a Redcoat officer—is missing, person who knew Harriet Tubman).

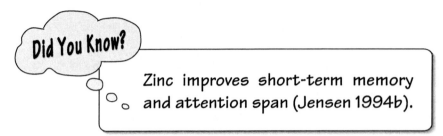

Did You Know?

Zinc improves short-term memory and attention span (Jensen 1994b).

Strategy 2

Poses and Gestures

In Brief

In lesson 1, students make facial expressions and brainstorm a list of vocabulary words to go along. In lesson 2 they use gestures to communicate the meaning of words. In lesson 3, students decide on the best gesture or pose to symbolize a concept or idea.

Objective

To help students learn to select the most effective gestures to communicate thoughts or ideas

Background

Physical gesture is the language of the body. Actors and dancers use their bodies to communicate stories and ideas. Body language is the first language of infants: they show us what they need and want long before they tell us.

Lesson 1: Say Smile!

Time

15 minutes

Materials

one large piece of writing paper per group

pencils or markers (preferable) for brainstorming

thought journals

thesauruses and dictionaries (optional)

Focus

Ask students to brainstorm words that describe feelings. Write the words on the board. Ask the students, "Is there more than one way to say sad or happy?" Write their ideas on the board.

Teach

Step 1: Tell students they are going to extend their vocabulary by brainstorming in groups and coming back to share. Remember, twenty-eight ideas are always better than one!

Step 2: Divide the class into groups of four or five students.

Step 3: Pick one student from each group to make the facial expression.

Step 4: Draw a smiley face on the board and then erase the mouth. Put in a mouth that is frowning. Have the acting student in each group imitate the face in different ways: frown, deep frown, eyes burrowed, lips scrunched, and so on.

Step 5: Ask students to write as many words as possible to describe the feeling on their actor's face. Let them use thesauruses and dictionaries, if such materials are available.

Step 6: Ask each group to designate a reporter who will read the group's list. As students read the words, write them down under the face you drew on the board. Discuss the various words: How are they different from one another? In what ways are they similar? Which words sound better? Do each mean the same thing?

Step 7: Repeat the activity twice more using a squiggly mouth, then a wide-open smiling mouth.

Step 8: On different days, repeat the lesson with physical actions (walking, sitting, speaking, and so on). Have students demonstrate various styles of each physical action and list synonyms on the chalkboard under a stick figure performing the same action. Use a thesaurus and dictionary to add unfamiliar words to the list, and have students act out those words as well (*traipse, trudge,* and so on).

Step 9: Ask students to copy the lists into their thought journals, and encourage them to refer to the lists when they are looking for a more creative or specific way to describe an action or feeling. Suggest that they add words to the list if they come across new words that have similar meanings.

Reflect

Ask students to talk about new words they learned doing this lesson. If none of the words was new, ask them to talk about their favorite words from the exercise.

Lesson 2: Meaning through Movement

Time

25 minutes (includes 10 minutes prep time)

Materials

five to ten index cards

one copy for each student of a vocabulary quiz sheet (see preparation)

Preparation

Make a quiz sheet of the current vocabulary list. List the words on one side and the meanings on the other in a different order so that students have to draw lines to match each word to its meaning. On each index card, write a vocabulary word on one side and the definition on the other side. Use vocabulary from any curriculum area, focusing on action or active words and avoiding proper nouns.

Focus

(adapted from Lazear 1991a)

Ask students to raise their hands if they have ever played charades. Ask them, "Can you describe how it's played? What do you like about the game?"

Note: Once when I used this strategy with my gifted class and invited teachers to refer any of their physically gifted students to the gifted class for the day, a teacher sent a student along with an apology: "He's very slow and I doubt he'll be able to keep up, but he is very coordinated and athletic." The student not only excelled in this vocabulary activity, he went on to get 100 percent on the vocabulary quiz after only twenty minutes of group physical study of the words!

Teach

Step 1: Hold up the first index card to show students the word or write it on the board.

Step 2: Invite a student to come up and look at the meaning on the back of the card. Tell the student he must make up an action or gesture that illustrates that meaning. You may want to act out the first word as an example.

Step 3: Ask students to stand by their desks and copy the movement or gesture without trying to guess the meaning of the word.

Step 4: Go through all the words the same way. Review all the motions from the beginning to be sure students remember the action that goes with each word.

Step 5: Ask students to take the vocabulary quiz.

Reflect

Ask students, "Is it easier or more difficult to learn words through actions? Why?" Discuss the answers as a class, then ask students to write down the new words they learned in their thought journals.

Lesson 3: Symbol Is in the Stance

Time

20 to 25 minutes (includes 5 to 10 minutes prep time)

Preparation

Select a current text from social studies, language arts, math, or science. Choose five concepts you want symbolized (for example, symbols for the southern colonies, the northern colonies, and the middle colonies; symbols for denominator and numerator; or symbols for abstract concepts and vocabulary such as *democracy, rebellion, independence*).

Focus

Ask students to suggest a physical pose that symbolizes the Pledge of Allegiance (hand across heart), *congratulations* (high five or thumbs up), and *I don't know* (shoulder shrug, outstretched hands with palms up).

Teach

Step 1: Divide the class into groups of four to five students each.

Step 2: List on the chalkboard the concepts you prepared. Assign each group one of the concepts and ask it to come up with a physical symbol (in other words, a brief movement or pose) of its assigned concept. Let students use their textbooks to help them get ideas.

Step 3: Give students five to ten minutes to work, depending on the complexity of the concepts you assigned. Then have the groups demonstrate their symbols for the class and explain why they think it accurately represents their concepts. For example, Maria's group is assigned the concept *sharecroppers*. They decide that, since sharecroppers do not own the property they farm, a good symbol would be empty pockets. They demonstrate their physical symbol for *sharecroppers* and explain its meaning.

Reflect

Ask students to discuss how turning concepts into symbols makes the concepts easier to understand.

Follow-up and Extension

Develop code gestures for classroom words such as *freeze, transition time, clean up,* or *pay attention*. Ask students to watch for you to make any of these gestures and copy whichever one it is. Let the symbols serve as reminders of the types of behavior students should engage in.

Applying the Strategy to Curriculum

1. Teach new vocabulary by acting out the meaning of the word, then asking students to write it down or memorize the definitions.

2. Let students develop physical gestures as symbols for some of the terms and concepts they are studying: for example, *patriotism* = hand over heart, *explorer* = hand shading eyes from sun with the other hand pointing forward, *magnification* = hands showing something growing larger.

Science

Develop lists of synonyms for scientific processes such as hypothesis, experiment, measure, and mix. Write the words on the board and, as a class, brainstorm synonyms.

Language Arts

1. As a group, brainstorm synonyms for vocabulary words by first acting out the word, then making lists to describe the action, pose, or expression.

2. As a class or reading group, develop poses to represent each character in the current reading.

3. Do an action or a pose (or have student volunteers do this), then ask the class to brainstorm similes to describe the action, for example, walking like an injured bird or dancing like a happy elephant.

Math

Have students develop physical symbols for geometric terms: *intersection* = crossed arms, *congruent* = mirror image with partner, *symmetry* = right and left arms moving together.

Social Studies

Have students divide into small groups and develop actions or poses to represent famous people.

Strategy 3

Body Graphing

In Brief

Students learn to use movement to understand grouping and sorting, to make human graphs, and to learn map skills.

Objective

To teach students how to use their bodies as learning aids

Background

Elementary students often have difficulty keeping still for long reading, writing, and paperwork assignments. This strategy capitalizes on their desire to get out of their seats and move to teach them sorting, graphing, and locating.

Lesson 1: Stand Up and Sort

Time

20 minutes

Focus

Ask students to name various animals. List the names they come up with on the chalkboard. Ask if any of the listed animals belong in the same group or family. Group those. Ask students, "How do you think scientists came up with the various groups or families? Why are tigers with cats and not with dogs or bears?" Allow a few minutes for them to discuss their answers. Ask students, "Are there any other times that we group things together? When?"

REMINDER When teaching this lesson or others that employ a lot of movement, call students up in small groups; otherwise your class will become chaotic.

Teach

Step 1: Tell students they are going to sort and group themselves.

Step 2: Ask students to stand by their desks and follow your instructions. Say, "Everyone who is wearing blue stand at the back of the room and everyone who is not wearing blue come to the front. Everyone wearing blue who also has on white, stand at the right side of the back of the room. Everyone wearing blue without any white, stand on the left side. Everyone in the front of the room who is wearing any white stand on the right side of the room. Everyone in the front of the room who is not wearing white, stand on the left. How many groups did we make?"

Step 3: Ask anyone who is wearing athletic shoes, tennis shoes, or high tops to sit down at their desks. Then ask everyone else to sit down.

Reflect

Ask students, "In what ways is it more fun to group and compare this way? In what ways is it more difficult?"

Lesson 2: Human Bar Graphs

Time

15 minutes

Materials

seven to ten blank index cards

a list of at least three characters from the current reading

Focus

Ask students to stand up if they like chocolate ice cream best. Vanilla? Strawberry? Ask if anyone could tell which flavor had the most votes. Ask them, "Was it hard or easy to tell?"

Teach

Step 1: Tell students they are going to use themselves to make quick bar graphs.

Step 2: Write *chocolate, vanilla,* and *strawberry* on three separate index cards. Ask for three volunteers to stand in front of the class and hold up the cards with their respective favorite flavors.

Step 3: Tell students, "Everyone who votes for chocolate line up in the chocolate line. Everyone who votes for vanilla line up in the vanilla line. Everyone who votes for strawberry line up in the strawberry line."

Step 4: Ask students to sit down at their desks and draw as best as they remember the human bar graph they just made. Demonstrate by drawing the following sketch on the chalkboard:

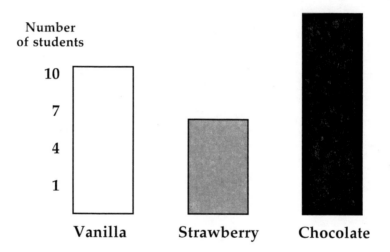

Lesson 3: Body as Geography

Time

15 minutes (includes 5 minutes prep time)

Materials

world or U.S. map

Preparation

Before starting this lesson, choose five to eight places you want students to be able to locate on a map.

Focus

Ask students to stand beside their desks and answer the following questions by pointing at their own bodies: "If you were a building, where would your roof be located?" (head) "Where would your basement be?" (feet)

Teach

Step 1: Stand at the front of the classroom and stretch your arms out. Ask students, "If I am the United States and my head is the North and my feet are the South, where is the West? Where is the East?" Have students stand and imitate you. You may need to face the same directions as students in order to help them keep right and left clear.

Step 2: Still standing with your arms stretched out, ask students to name the states that belong on the right hand (the West Coast). Then ask which states belong on the left hand (the East Coast).

Step 3: Ask students, "Which states go across our feet? Across our heads? Which belong in the middle?"

Step 4: If your focus is global geography, ask students to pretend you are the world, then ask students to name the location of the North Pole (your head), Antarctica (your feet), the equator (stomach), the Tropic of Cancer (chest or neck), Tropic of Capricorn (knees), and so on.

Reflect

Ask students, "Is it easier or harder to learn geography this way? Why?"

Follow-up and Extension

You can regularly use the human sorting or graphing technique to divide the class into teams for physical education or into small cooperative groups.

Applying the Strategy to Curriculum

Reteach lesson 1 using students' opinions about a current event, something that just happened or is about to happen in a language arts reading, or a social studies unit. Put people who agree with the stated opinion on one end of the line, and people who disagree on the other end. The middle is for those who cannot decide, and in-between the middle and each end is for students who are close to deciding one way or the other. Once they get used to doing this exercise, they can do it quickly, providing a welcome quick break from sitting without completely disrupting the class.

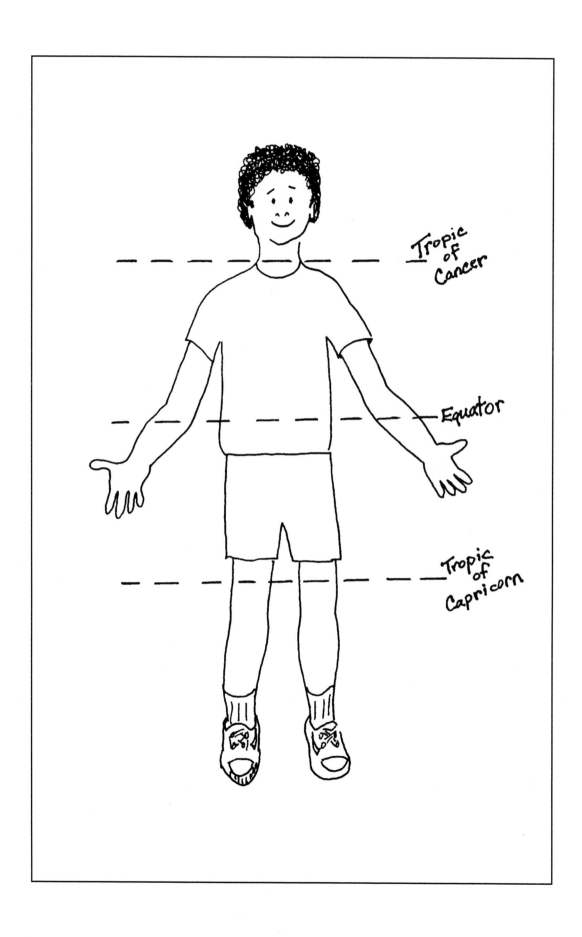

Science

1. Ask students to form a line graph based on their hypotheses on the outcome of an experiment.

2. Give students index cards with names of chemical compounds such as H_2O, then sort the class based on individual components, number of electrons, or whether the compound is a solid, liquid, or gas.

Language Arts

1. Make a human bar graph by asking students to vote on their favorite characters from the current reading.

2. Form human bar graphs to vote on various options for the end of the story.

3. Reteach lesson 1 using vocabulary words on index cards. Sort by prefix, suffix, number of syllables, or part of speech.

Math

1. Bar graph anything: favorite television shows, last movie seen or rented; favorite school subjects; students' ages; birth times or months.

2. Reteach lesson 1 with geometric shapes. Prepare a class set of thirty index cards, six each with a picture of a square, rectangle, triangle, rhombus, and parallelogram. Pass them out randomly to students, then ask them to sort themselves based on your instructions. Separate the front and back of the room by sides—shapes with three sides go to the front, shapes with four sides go to the back. Then separate by angles: all equal angles go to the right side of the room, unequal angles go to the left side of the room. Have shapes with equal sides sit down at their desks and shapes that are symmetrical stand on one foot.

Social Studies

1. Form human bar graphs by asking students to vote on why they think particular historical events happened, for example, "What started the Civil War? Why did settlers move West?"

2. Make up index cards that say *slave, white colonist, American Indian, freed African American,* and *sharecropper.* Ask for student volunteers to sort themselves into a line based on amount of freedom. Allow for discussion and debate.

3. Use body geography to teach the locations of continents, oceans, latitude and longitude, countries, and so on.

Strategy 4

Pantomime and Dance

In Brief

Students learn to use movement to communicate actions, identity, or settings, then apply what they've learned to telling a short story.

Objective

To encourage students to use movement and acting to tell a story

Background

Pantomime and dance are two easy physical ways to tell a story. We often test student comprehension by asking them to summarize or paraphrase something they have read. This activity gives a new twist to that assignment by allowing students to tell a story kinesthetically through acting or a dance.

Lesson 1: What Am I?

Time

25 minutes (including 5 minutes prep time)

Materials

copy of the pantomime ideas

Preparation

Make one copy of the pantomime ideas on page 95. Cut the copies along the lines.

Focus

Ask students, "Has anyone here ever seen a mime or know what a mime is? What do they look like? What do they do?"

Teach

Step 1: Tell students they are going to perform some very simple mime actions in groups.

Step 2: Divide the class into six groups.

Step 3: Give one of the activity 1 action cards to each group.

Step 4: Tell the groups to work five minutes to develop the pantomime, making the action, identity, or setting on their cards
recognizable to the rest of the class. All members of each group
should take part in the pantomime, though some might have
to play objects instead of people.

Step 5: Ask each group to perform without sound and have the class
try to guess the action, identity, or setting.

Lesson 2: Mime Movies

Time

25 minutes (including 5 minutes prep time)

Materials

one copy of each of the activity 2 Pantomime Ideas

Focus

Ask students, "Remember the mime acts we did? What was that like?
Was it easy to imitate one thing? Do you remember how you used your
bodies to imitate not only actions, but also objects?"

Teach

Step 1: Explain to the class that they are going to mime some simple
stories in small groups.

Step 2: Divide the class into groups of four or five.

Step 3: Give each group one of the activity 2 cards.

Step 4: Give students about ten minutes to practice. Tell them that this
time, they can mime their activity or turn the story into a dance
with rhythm and music but no words.

Step 5: Have class performances.

Reflect

Ask students to discuss how it is more enjoyable and more difficult to
summarize a story this way.

Follow-up and Extension

Use lesson 2 whenever you want to check students' understanding of
a historic time line or a plot.

Applying the Strategy to Curriculum

Note: Any pantomime can be turned into a full-blown performance
with the addition of a little background music and costumes.

Activity 1 Your group is a cave. Find a way to show that you are a cave.	**Activity 1** Your group is a ferry. Find a way to show that you are a ferry.	**Activity 1** Your group is a group of firefighters. Find a way to show what you are without props.
Activity 1 Your group is the ocean. Find a way to imitate the waves and flow of the ocean.	**Activity 1** Your group is a football team. Using only the small space in the front of the classroom, find an action you can do that imitates a football team.	**Activity 1** Your group is a machine. Find a way to look like a machine at work.
Activity 2 You have a person working on a machine. The machine is ticking away and the person's tie gets caught in the gears. The person cannot reach the button to turn off the machine, so finally has to cut off the tie.	**Activity 2** You are a group of people waiting at a bus stop. You are looking about, checking watches, reading. One of you begins to sing (remember, no sound) and the rest join in.	**Activity 2** One of you is a driver and the rest are a vehicle going over a rough bumpy road. The ride gets worse and worse; finally, you fall apart and the driver is left with no car.
Activity 2 One person is in a boat on the ocean. The waves are growing higher and higher. The boat capsizes and the person struggles then drowns in the ocean.	**Activity 2** A person goes into an elevator. At each floor the doors open and the person looks out and shakes his head no; it's the wrong floor. At the roof the person finally gets off the elevator and flies away.	**Activity 2** Your group is made up of one firefighter and a fire. The firefighter turns on the hose and is winning the battle against the flames. Then the hose runs out of water, the flames kick up, and the firefighter flees.

Multltiple Intelligences Made Easy © 1999 Zephyr Press, Inc., Tucson, Arizona

Pick a group of students to develop a mime or dance from an event you are studying in social studies or a character you are reading about in language arts. See if the class can guess what story or event the group is portraying.

Science

Divide the class into small groups and have each group create a pantomime that portrays a different mechanical or scientific process or property, such as gravity or ropes and pulleys.

Language Arts

1. Have students mime a character, a character's dilemma, a setting, or a short plot.
2. As a class, try to boil down a story to its bare bones: beginning, middle, and end. Then divide the class into groups to re-create the story in brief pantomimes or dances.

Math

Divide the class into small groups and ask them each to make up a dance or pantomime that shows symmetry, asymmetry, congruence, parallel lines, right angles, and so on.

Social Studies

1. Ask student volunteers to retell a historical event without using words.
2. Have your students create a dance that feels like the Underground Railroad, the cotton pickers, or the gold rush. Pick some classical music. Ask a student to provide a gesture or action that represents the thing she is portraying. Have a small group dance the motion to the music. Allow additional students to add various elements that relate to the story (such as a plantation owner sitting in a rocking chair on the porch or a foreman with a whip).

Strategy 5

Mini Simulations

In Brief

You choose a learning objective and use this strategy to create a quickie simulation for students.

Time

varies based on learning objective (including 5 to 10 minutes prep time)

Objective

To put together variations of instant and easy simulations to accomplish a particular learning objective

Background

A simulation is an activity designed to help students empathize with a particular historical person's or literary character's dilemma. Many elaborate simulations software (*Oregon Trail* is a popular one) and books exists. These learning units teach a great deal and students enjoy them a great deal, but it can be difficult to find time for long, drawn-out simulations.

Lesson 1: Mini Simulation

Preparation

Ask yourself what you want to accomplish with simulation. For example, "I want my students to empathize with American Indians when they were pushed out of their homelands"; "I want my students to understand how a revolution begins—the feelings and frustration that power such a change." "I want my students to understand what it would feel like to be unable to use their hands."

Teach

The way to create a mini simulation is to decide upon an objective and then find a way to re-create similar feelings, on a smaller scale and for a shorter period of time, in your students. For example, if you want students to understand some of the emotions people felt during slavery, label students as slaves and owners based on the color or length of their hair, then tell the slaves they have to do homework for themselves and their owners. Don't actually make them do the homework; just make the announcement and let the information sink in before engaging in a reality-check. If you want them to understand American Indians losing their homeland, tell them fifteen new and special students are going to be joining the class and current students will need to move their chairs and desks into a small back area. If you want them to understand how it feels to have a disability, get them to refrain from using their hands, eyes, or ears for a period of time.

> **REMINDER**
>
> Simulations can arouse powerful emotions. When I used the exercise to explore the meaning of rebellion, my students' displeasure quickly grew from grumbling and chair scraping to standing and yelling. I suggest that you describe what's going to happen and why before beginning a simulation, watch students' faces and actions very closely, and end the simulation before the most rambunctious or sensitive students begin to lose control.

Reflect

The crucial element of any mini simulation is reflection. Ask students what kinds of feelings they had. Write some of the key words from their responses on the board. Ask them how their experiences might relate to the experiences of those you were trying to emulate. Create a Venn diagram to compare the two experiences and help students understand that their own experiences were much less real or intense. Ask students to write or draw in their thought journals what they learned by going through this simulation.

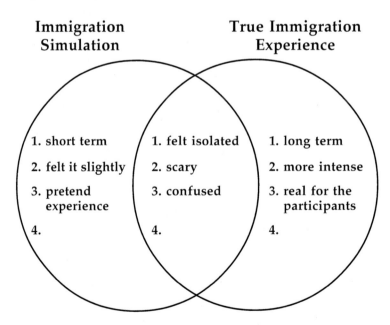

Immigration Simulation | True Immigration Experience

Immigration Simulation:
1. short term
2. felt it slightly
3. pretend experience
4.

(overlap):
1. felt isolated
2. scary
3. confused
4.

True Immigration Experience:
1. long term
2. more intense
3. real for the participants
4.

Follow-up and Extension

Use this strategy whenever you want to deepen students' empathy with characters or historical events.

4

Visual-Spatial Intelligence

Visual-spatial intelligence focuses on powers of observation and the ability to design and understand the space around us. Architects, artists, designers, explorers, and map makers use visual-spatial skills to breathe life into artistic and functional ideas and concepts, to record life experiences, and to find their ways. Children are no strangers to the imagination, so visual learning comes relatively easy to them.

The strategies in this chapter help children explore their visual-spatial intelligence by honing their observational skills; by helping them use their inner eyes to see and understand more clearly the world around them. Any time learning involves the use of pictures, images, or visual imagination, visual-spatial intelligence is being exercised. In addition to the strategies shared here, you can add visual smarts to the regular curriculum in a delightfully large number of ways. Try studying historic artwork, watching movies and videos, and making sculptures and paintings. Try imitating folk art or designing sets for classroom plays and productions. Let students visualize their way to better learning!

Strategy 1

Activating Your Imagination

In Brief

Students learn to harness their visual imaginations as a learning tool.

Objective

To teach students to use the pictures in their heads to "see" and experience events or to review study material

Background

The technique of creative visualization—using your imagination to see something—is used to enhance memory and retain information. The visual areas of the brain, in the right hemisphere, are better able to retain and recall information; visualizing events or information in our minds gives us a memory as if the thing actually happened to us. Creative visualization capitalizes on this phenomenon to help students learn better and retain more. It is also a useful way to teach about empathy and attention to detail, and can be used with sequencing and prewriting or prereading exercises.

Lesson 1: The Balloon

Time

10 minutes

Materials

thought journals

Focus

Ask students if they like to daydream. Ask for volunteers to share favorite daydreams. Ask them, "Do you ever choose what you're going to dream about before you begin daydreaming?"

Teach

Step 1: Tell students they are going to practice using their visual imaginations to see pictures in their heads, then they are going to learn how to use those pictures to study.

Step 2: Ask students to sit up straight and relax their shoulders and arms. As a class, take two or three deep breaths. Ask students to concentrate and listen quietly to what you say.

Step 3: Tell students, "I want you to see the color red in your mind. In your mind, make a balloon and fill it with red. Picture the balloon floating right in front of your eyes. Make it grow and grow and grow, then make it shrink and shrink and shrink."

Step 4: Tell your students, "Now, open your eyes and draw what you pictured. Draw more than one picture if you have to."

Step 5: Ask students to share what they saw, if anything. It is interesting to note how children visualize the same thing differently from others. Some will picture the balloon rising up and maybe even popping, while others will visualize a paintbrush filling in the balloon with red. Some will not be successful the first time they try visualization. Explain that it's okay not to see anything, and that they will have more chances.

Step 6: Practice the visualization two or three more times on different days before transferring the strategy to your curriculum. You may vary this basic visualization: you might change the color of the balloon to blue, to green, to checkerboard black-and-white; have the balloon float up to the ceiling or down to the floor; visualize making it big enough to sit on and ride over the school. You might try other visualizations, as well: a ball bouncing from desk to desk, students' hair growing longer and longer, or the floor turning into Jell-O.

Reflect

Answer the following question as a class: "Why is this experience different for every student?"

Lesson 2: Movies in Our Heads

Time

15 minutes (includes 5 minutes prep time)

Materials

thought journals

Preparation

Select a moment from a current social studies unit or a scene from the current language arts reading. If possible, look at a picture or drawing to get ideas for the visualization. Jot down notes to help you re-create the scene orally for the class.

Teach

Step 1: Ask students to sit up tall and relax their shoulders and arms.

Step 2: As a class, take two or three deep breaths.

Step 3: Ask students to concentrate and listen quietly to what you say. Describe the scene you chose. Ask students to picture the scene in their minds, and ask them particular questions to encourage detailed visualizations. Following are examples of visualizations:

Imagine a cobblestone street in Boston in 1774. Imagine a group of men crossing the street one at a time and entering an inn through the back door. They are looking all around and trying to appear calm, but they look worried—as if they don't want to be seen. Can you recognize any of the men in the group? What are they doing?

Imagine that you are a Mohawk hunting deer in the forest near your home. You come out of the forest to the seashore, and suddenly in front of you is a great ship. White-skinned people are getting off the ship, and men, women, and children are saying words you do not understand. You run quickly back to your tribe to tell the news.

Imagine that you've just got in a glass elevator with Willy Wonka, who owns the local chocolate factory. He's a strange man and your stomach is nervous. He asks you to push a button and you feel the floor move beneath you. You feel yourself going up . . . up . . . up . . . through the ceiling and finally, smash! You crash out into the sky!

Step 4: After the imagining time, ask students to write or draw in their thought journals about what they saw.

Reflect

Ask students, "How did you like the visualization technique? Were you successful at seeing? How is it different from hearing or reading the story?"

Follow-up and Extension

Just before a test, ask students to visualize knowing all the answers. Have students imagine their hands gliding down the page and understanding every question. Ask them to imagine how satisfied they'll feel after completing the test.

Applying the Strategy to Curriculum

Science

Use visualization to increase students' understandings of scientific concepts. Following is an example of a visualization to help students understand the size of a cell:

> *Imagine yourselves shrinking . . . shrinking to the size of a pencil . . . then to the size of a pin . . . then to the size of a tiny, tiny seed . . . then smaller until you are the size of a flake of skin . . . then smaller until you can walk on that flake and begin to see the edges of cells like rounded bumps on the surface of the flake.*

To help students learn about gravity, have them visualize landing on various planets to feel how the gravity changes. To help them learn about light, use visualizations about reflection, refraction, and absorption. You might have them imagine they are riding a wave of light energy. It travels in a straight line unless it hits something. Then what happens? What if it hits water? A mirror? A prism?

Language Arts

1. Have students visualize scenes in the current reading selection.

Did You Know? In *Picture This*, Laura Rose (1989) writes: "For those of us who read well and with pleasure, a crucial point may be hard to believe: students who do not read well or who read without pleasure are probably not getting a mental picture of what is happening in the stories they read. And, without the ability to visualize and bring forth images, they will remain as they are, weak readers" (11).

2. Before assigning students to write an original story, do a visualization exercise on the topic or setting. Frequent use of this exercise will help them develop greater descriptive abilities.

3. Use visualization as an editing technique. Working one-on-one with students or dividing the class into pairs, ask students to visualize the topic they wrote about while you read the writing back. Afterward, ask them, "Do you think the story flows well? How does it look in your head? Were your descriptions detailed enough to help you see good pictures in your head?"

4. Teach students to use visualization to learn and practice their spelling words. Ask them to close their eyes and imagine the word appearing letter by letter while you read the letters to the class. Or ask students to visualize the word as a picture and superimpose the spelling of the word over the scene.

5. Do a visualization of a nature scene before writing haiku or other nature poetry. Following are several examples:

> *You are sitting outside . . . There is a slight, cool breeze. Leaves are floating down from the trees. The ground is moist. A bug crawls over your hand. What do you smell? What do you hear? What else do you see?*

> *Rain and wind are beating against your windowpane. You step outside. Trees are bending. What do you see when you look down? What do you see when you look up?*

Math

Assign a work sheet of word problems and spend time as a class visualizing each problem before students start working individually on solutions.

Social Studies

1. Re-create any scene from history using creative visualization. Choose the scene based on your learning objective for the lesson: to understand the motivation for the Revolutionary War, to empathize with the plight of American Indians, or to understand the thrill of discovery, and so on.

2. Use visualization to help students create an imaginary time line by asking them to visualize each distinct step leading up to a particular moment in history.

3. To help students learn geography, ask them to visualize flying over the world and looking down at all the countries, continents, states, oceans, and other geographic features.

Physical Education

Remind students to visualize success: for example, before going up to bat, visualize hitting the ball; before the other person throws the ball, visualize catching it.

Strategy 2

Three-Dimensional Paper Shapes

In Brief

Students use trial and error to design a pattern for making a cube out of construction paper.

Time

20 minutes

Objectives

To introduce students to the differences between two and three dimensions

To teach students how to turn one dimension into the other

Background

The ability to organize two- and three-dimensional space is one of the central components of visual-spatial intelligence. With this strategy, students also practice concepts of design and trial and error.

Lesson 1: Cubism

Materials

two or three pieces for each student of 5-by-7-inch construction paper

scissors

rulers

glue and tape

Focus

Roll a piece of construction paper into a cylinder. Ask students for suggestions on how to add a top and bottom (tape circles on the end, make circles with tabs that can be glued on, and so on).

Teach

Step 1: Tell students that you want them to design a pattern for making a three-dimensional box—a cube—out of the construction paper. Explain that a pattern is a flat piece of paper with the cut, fold, and glue lines drawn in.

Step 2: Ask students to work independently, though they should feel free to discuss and share their progress with other students.

Step 3: Pass out rulers, scissors, construction paper (enough for a few tries), and scissors or glue.

Step 4: Tell students that their patterns should be all in one piece; that is, all the parts of the box—top, bottom, sides—should be connected.

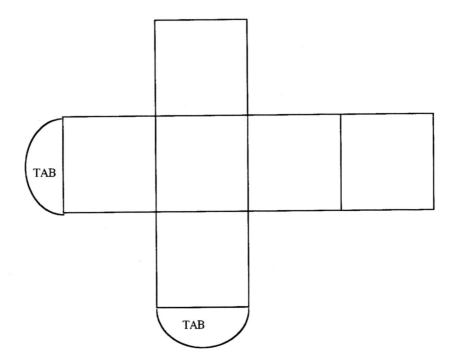

Step 5: Allow students about fifteen minutes to work on patterns until they find one with which they are happy.

Step 6: Ask one or two students to draw their patterns on the chalkboard. Ask the volunteers to try to explain how they arrived at their ideas.

Reflect

Ask students, "Could you use the same pattern to make a bigger-sized box? What kind of adjustments would you have to make? What about using the pattern to make a rectangular box?"

Follow-up and Extension

Encourage students to experiment making patterns for various shapes: pyramids, rectangular boxes, and so on.

Applying the Strategy to Curriculum

Make mobiles or dioramas from the three-dimensional constructions. Mobiles can use three-dimensional shapes to experiment with balance (science) or to display information about study materials (each shape representing a different character, story element, or American Indian tribe, with information written on the various sides).

Science

To teach about volume, make patterns for a variety of shapes and experiment to see which one will hold more popcorn, styrofoam peanuts, or another light material that is not likely to make the shape fall apart.

Language Arts

1. Make 6-by-6-inch paper boxes out of construction paper. Once students have the pattern but before they glue or tape the box together, use each side to list book report information: author and title, summary, main character, key turning point, two illustrations.
2. Read *Sadako and the Thousand Cranes* by Eleanor Coerr. Discuss origami and learn how to make a crane.

Math

1. Use students' construction paper cubes to teach them about area, perimeter, and volume.
2. Look at flat patterns and have students guess what shapes each one will fold into. You can either draw your own patterns or get some from the school district psychologist, who may have access to patterns on psychological and aptitude tests.

Social Studies

Teach a lesson on the origami tradition.

Strategy 3

Contour Drawing

In Brief

Students learn contour drawing—a technique that requires them to pay close attention to the object being drawn—to increase attention span and aid learning.

Objectives

To exercise the right hemisphere of students' brains

To help students learn to draw by fostering their ability to see the edges and lines of pictures and objects

Background

Contour drawing has been a staple of art instruction for centuries. Only recently, however, with increased understanding of the workings of the right and left brain, have we begun to fully appreciate the value of contour drawing outside of art instruction, as a technique that increases the ability to observe closely and see as an artist sees.

Lesson 1: Hand Drawing Hand

Time

40 minutes (includes 10 minutes prep time)

Materials

white or newsprint paper for drawing

tape

pencils or black markers (preferable)

Preparation

Write the following rules either on an overhead projector transparency or a poster:

Rules of Contour Drawing

1. Choose an item that has lots of lines and detail.
2. Start drawing from the center of the object and work outward slowly, trying to draw in every detail.

3. Never lift your pencil or marker from the paper. Just draw a continuous line—it's okay to overlap.

4. **No erasing!!** The eraser is the left brain trying to take over!

5. Work without talking for at least ten minutes straight.

Focus

Ask students, "Who would like to learn how to draw?" Tell them that by learning how to contour draw, they will be exercising a part of the brain that is best at drawing or learning to draw. Explain that if they exercise that part often enough—and if they practice—they may learn to draw very well.

Teach

Step 1: Explain that this activity is called *contour drawing* because students draw the contours, or edges, of things.

Step 2: Give them the following instructions for the first ten-minute drawing session:

Tape your piece of drawing paper onto your desk. I want you to draw your own hand, so put your nondrawing hand into a tight fist with the palm facing up. You're going to draw your hand without looking at the piece of paper and without ever lifting your pencil or marker. Just follow the lines of your hand with your eyes and copy the movement with your pencil.

Start in the middle and slowly follow every line. Try to get every wrinkle, every edge. Concentrate on the wrinkles and edges; don't try to draw the fingernails.

Step 3: Walk around and observe while students work, reminding them to keep their eyes on their hands and their pencils on their papers.

Step 4: Their drawings will look a lot like scribbles and very little like their own hands. Explain that that's fine as long as they are drawing slowly and trying to show lots of detail and wrinkles. You want them to be really engaged in looking, concentrating, and examining the edges and lines of their hands.

Step 5: At the close of the exercise, ask students, "Do you think your right brain got exercise while you were contour drawing? Why?" Explain that there are clues that can help them figure out whether they were using their right brains: ten minutes feels like half an hour, or half an hour feels like ten minutes (they lose track of time); you stop talking and don't want to hear anyone else talk (words are left-brain mode); you get lost in the work of drawing.

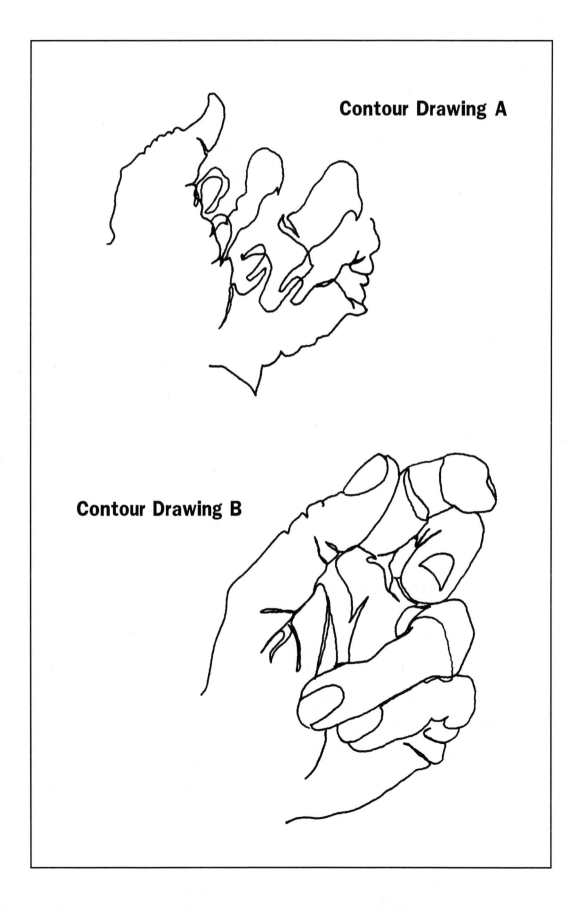

Contour Drawing A

Contour Drawing B

Step 6: Start a second contour drawing session. Have students draw their hands again, palm up, but this time with some of their fingers folded into the palm. Tell them to remember to draw in one continuous line, starting in the middle. This time they can look at the paper, but they should try to spend most of the time focused on the lines and wrinkles of the hand. They should draw the fingernails last.

Step 7: The human hand can be drawn over and over, but for variety try contour drawing one of the following objects (notice that all are somewhat organic and full of lines and detail):

a tennis shoe (facing front to see all those wonderful laces)

a leafy plant

a crumpled piece of paper

a set of keys

a crumpled sweater or jacket

a semi-folded sock

Reflect

As a class, discuss the answer to the following question: "Following the edges of something, do you notice anything that went unnoticed before?"

Lesson 2: Advanced Contour Drawing

Time

30 to 35 minutes (includes 5 to 10 minutes prep time)

Materials

List of contour drawing guidelines from lesson 1

white or newsprint paper for drawing

tape

pencils or black markers (preferable)

textbook with pictures

Preparation

Choose an illustration or photograph that relates to a current unit of study in history or science and make photocopies for the class.

Focus

Ask students, "Do you suppose we could use contour drawing to learn history or science? How?" Review the rules of contour drawing and do a warm-up activity: have students contour draw their hands without looking at the paper or draw a picture from the textbook by looking at it upside down.

Teach

Step 1: Give students ten to fifteen minutes to contour draw the picture you chose. Remind them again to start in the middle, draw one continuous line, look at the paper only once in a while, and concentrate on getting all the lines and detail.

Step 2: After they're done drawing, assign them to write labels or captions for their drawings.

Reflect

Ask students, "How does contour drawing help you see the picture better?" Discuss students' ideas and encourage them to understand that contour drawing helps them see more of the details of the picture.

Follow-up and Extension

Give contour drawing as a homework assignment: Have students draw plants, shoes, animals from a book, the bathroom sink, and so on.

Applying the Strategy to Curriculum

Science

1. Contour draw objects from the current science unit. Remember that detailed objects with lots of lines and a variety of shapes (such as scientific tools) make the best contour drawings. Once the drawings are completed, assign students to research the names of and make labels for all the parts.
2. Contour draw a portrait of a famous scientist.

Language Arts

1. Contour draw illustrations from the current reading.
2. Find in magazines, encyclopedias, or books pictures that evoke the characters or setting of the current reading; have students contour draw the pictures.

Math

Have students contour draw their hands or other objects, then assign them to figure out ways to measure the length of the lines. Compare students' ideas and actual measurements. Do they vary wildly, or are they all within a range? Chart the results of the measurements.

Social Studies

1. Contour draw any detailed picture from the current social studies unit. Good places to look for pictures include textbooks, library books, or encyclopedias. As a warm-up, have students draw the picture upside down.

2. Contour draw pictures of tools, clothing, or modes of transportation common to the time period being studied. As a class, create a poster or brochure of the time period illustrated with contour drawings.

3. Assign students to contour draw a portrait of a famous person.

4. After students have completed a contour drawing of an object or scene from a particular time period, have them cut it out in the shape of a postcard. Ask them to pretend they live during the time period, and have them write a letter on the back of the card.

Strategy 4

Seeing Like a Map Maker

In Brief

Students learn about perspective, ratio, and proportion through making a map of the classroom.

Objectives

To teach students how to represent objects from a birds-eye view

To teach students to use the bird's-eye skill to design and read maps

Background

Map makers and navigators have the ability to find their way around in a three-dimensional world using two-dimensional maps and acute spatial sense. It's as if they can see from above. This strategy helps students uncover and develop this skill in themselves.

Lesson 1: Bird's-Eye View

Time

30 minutes (includes 10 minutes prep time)

Materials

thought journals

maps from books, old street maps, or atlases

Preparation

Gather maps for students to study.

Focus

Ask students to close their eyes and breathe deeply two or three times. Ask them to imagine themselves floating above the room and looking down at themselves. Ask them to pay attention to what they see from this perspective: Can they see their feet? Legs? Shoulders? Faces?

Teach

Step 1: When students open their eyes, tell them to draw in their thought journals what they could see of their bodies and desks from above.

Step 2: Discuss as a class what was visible (tops of their heads, desk tops, and so on).

Step 3: As a class, draw a simple representation of a person sitting at a desk, as seen from above (circle for the top of the head, a square for the desk).

Step 4: Give students five to ten minutes to design in their thought journals two or three more simple bird's-eye representations of objects in the classroom or at school.

Step 5: Have students examine the maps you brought in—either individually or in small groups, depending on how many maps you were able to find—and share with the class what kinds of symbols and drawings map makers use to represent objects.

Reflect

Ask students, "Are maps always drawn from a bird's-eye view? What other ways are there to draw maps?" Explain that there are maps that represent objects as three-dimensional, or will use symbols instead of an aerial view (especially common in atlases). Discuss as a class the importance of using legends and recognizable symbols in map making.

Lesson 2: Make a Map

Time

25 minutes

Materials

rulers, yardsticks, or tape measures

one for each student of 8½-by-11-inch or larger white construction paper or newsprint

Focus

Ask a student volunteer to draw on the chalkboard a bird's-eye representation of a person sitting at a desk. Ask one or two other students to come up to the board and draw other classroom objects (sinks, cabinets, tables, and so on).

Teach

Step 1: Ask a student to measure the width and length of the classroom either with a tape measure, yardstick, or by pacing off the distance. Ask the same student to pace off or measure one desk or table.

Step 2: Write the measurements or estimates on the chalkboard.

Step 3: Explain to students that map makers draw maps in proportion to what they are drawing. Tell them that the definition of proportion is a comparative relation between things. Draw a large rectangle on the board. Then draw a small square, a small rectangle whose proportions do not match the large rectangle, and a small rectangle with the same proportions as the large rectangle.

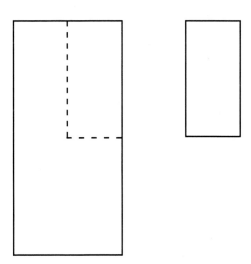

Step 4: Ask students, "Which of the small shapes has the same proportions as the large rectangle?"

Step 5: Tell them that you don't expect exact measurements, but that you want them to work individually to make a map of the classroom showing the proportions of the room and including desks, pupils, sinks, and cabinets. Give them fifteen minutes to work on this project.

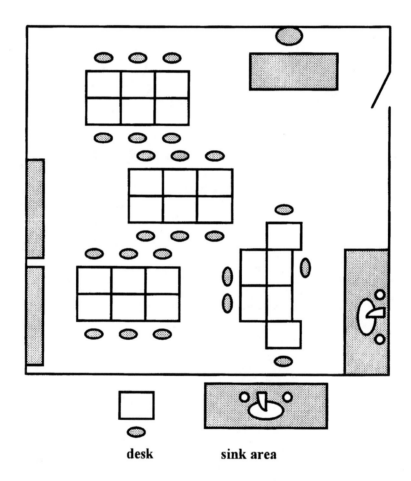

desk   sink area

Reflect

Ask students, "Were you able to fit all the objects into your map? What was difficult about making a map of the room?" Ask for student volunteers to share their maps with the class.

Follow-up and Extension

As a homework or independent project, have students draw maps of their homes or the block they live on, including legends.

Applying the Strategy to Curriculum

Review and discuss any maps used in social studies, geography, or language arts materials (sometimes stories include maps of the setting). Draw some of the map symbols on the chalkboard. Discuss what kind of perspective the map maker chose to use to represent the setting: bird's eye or other? Does the perspective work well for the kind of information the map maker wants to convey?

Before a field trip, ask students to pretend they are map makers scouting a location before making a map. Tell them they can either make notes of particular details during the field trip or simply pay attention to the layout of the place. When they come back to school or the next day, allow students time to draw maps of the location.

Science

1. Before conducting an experiment or cooking a recipe, give students their materials and a list of steps and have them lay out everything they think will help them conduct the experiment most efficiently. Explain that scientists always plan in advance and set up all materials before starting an experiment.

2. After a field trip to the zoo, have students draw a map of the zoo with the locations of the various animals, or study a map of the zoo before going and ask students to remember where their favorite animals are located in relation to others.

3. Make or study diagrams of the insides of tools and machines. Ask students how reading assembly instructions can be like reading a map.

Language Arts

When a setting is particularly well described, assign students to make a map of the story's main locations. *James and the Giant Peach* by Roald Dahl, for example, is a destination book that lends itself to map review and map making.

Math

1. Teach the students about ratio. Have them measure the table tops and re-create the proportions on paper.

2. Create a hidden treasure map that leads to a treasure you have hidden in the schoolyard or classroom, using proportion instead of providing the actual measurements, for example, one pace = a half-inch.

Social Studies

1. Have students create a book of personal maps—both drawn and traced or collected: my home, my neighborhood, places I have visited, my city, state, my country.

2. Have students draw maps from scratch or with tracing paper to understand geography.

Strategy 5

Visual Symbols

In Brief

This strategy teaches students how to interpret the meaning of symbols. In the second lesson they develop their own symbols, and finally practice what they have learned by interpreting the symbolic imagery of political cartoons.

Objective

To introduce students to the use of visual symbols to interpret information, increase retention, and build comprehension

Background

Visual symbolism is found throughout history in all cultures and is probably the precursor to written language. Visual imagery is relatively universal, and visual symbols can still be found everywhere today, from advertising logos to signs to computer screens.

Did You Know?

Throughout Europe, where a lot of people speaking a variety of languages converge in a relatively small geographic area, street signs use symbols instead of words to convey information.

Lesson 1: Interpreting and Using Symbols

Time

35 minutes (includes 5 minutes prep time)

Materials

one copy for each student of Visual Symbols handout

thought journals

Preparation

Photocopy the Visual Symbols handout or copy it onto an overhead transparency or the chalkboard. Review the key on page 122 so you can help students understand the symbols.

Focus

Explain to the class that a symbol is a picture or image that brings to mind something else. Draw a dollar sign on the board, and ask what this symbol makes them think about. Draw a McDonald's-style *M* and ask the same question.

Teach

Step 1: Ask the class to turn their attention to the Visual Symbols on the handout (or on the board or overhead).

Step 2: Ask students, "Can anyone tell me what those first and second symbols might represent?" Talk about how some symbols are more obvious than others.

Step 3: Ask students, "Can anyone guess the meaning for the third symbol?" Students will find this symbol more difficult to interpret because it doesn't mean exactly what they might think. Lead them to the correct answer (clouds) and explain that the symbol comes from the way that clouds sometimes form flat shapes and outline mountains.

Step 4: Tell students, "When these three symbols are combined as they are at the end of the first line, they form a sentence that is a visual poem. Can you figure out what the poem says?" Spend some time guessing, and lead them to the answer: "An eagle lives above the clouds."

Step 5: Ask students, "Are any of the rest of these symbols familiar? Have you ever seen any of them before? Where?"

Step 6: Go through the rest of the symbols together and guess what they might mean.

<table>
<tr><td colspan="2" align="center">KEY</td></tr>
</table>

1. eagle	6. sleep
2. home	7. waves
3. clouds	8. hello or friends
4. "An eagle lives above the clouds."	9. road
5. village or community	10. mountains

Step 7: Have students select a few symbols and put then together (either by redrawing them or by cutting and pasting) to create a design or a visual poem. Ask them to write a translation to their poem beneath the design.

Step 8: Tell students, "This week I want you to pay attention to symbols all around you at school and at home. Find examples of other symbols to share with the class. When you notice them in our books, raise your hand and point them out for all of us to see." Brainstorm as a class places in and out of school to look for symbols.

Reflect

Ask students to answer the following question in their thought journals: "How does a visual symbol explain something easier or better than words?"

Lesson 2: Making Our Own Symbols

Time

25 minutes (includes 5 minutes prep time)

Materials

newsprint or white paper for drawing

Preparation

Copy the following list of words on the chalkboard or an overhead transparency:

art	brother	father	fall	fast
teacher	P.E.	summer	anger	follow
winter	mother	play	math	beautiful
friend	travel	food	motion	ugly
drive	pet store	clothing	happy	light
turn	sister	spring	slow	wet

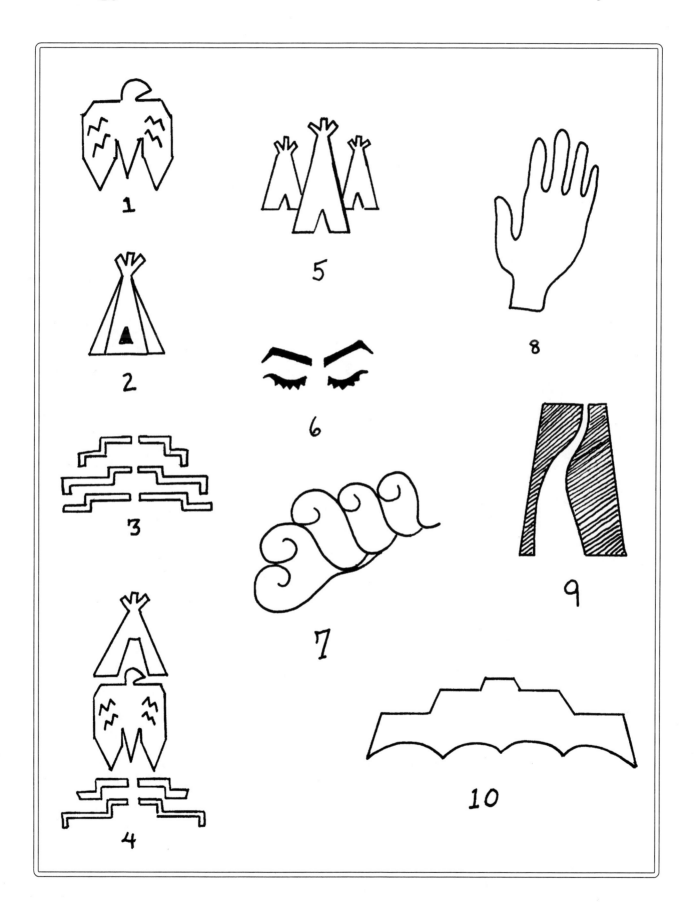

Focus

Ask students, "What is a symbol? Are there many different kinds? Are symbols complete drawings that look just like the object or action?" Allow some class discussion so that students understand that a symbol can be very simple and that it only has to provide a clue to the action or object it represents.

Teach

Step 1: Tell students, "On the chalkboard or overhead is a list of thirty words that you can turn into symbols. I want you to pick out two or three words for which to create symbols." Let students take their time to choose.

Step 2: Have students spend fifteen minutes sketching symbol ideas into their thought journals, then ask them to share one idea with the class by drawing it on the chalkboard or overhead.

Lesson 3: Editorial Cartoons

Time

35 minutes (includes 10 minutes prep time)

Materials

old newspapers, with opinion pages and five to ten editorial cartoons

Focus

Remind students that a symbol is a picture or image that brings to mind something else. Explain that through-out history people have used symbols to share their opinions. Draw a flower in a circle and draw a line through it. Ask them, "How does this artist feel about flowers?"

Teach

Step 1: Divide the class into groups of three or four.

Step 2: Explain that one good place to look for people expressing their opinions with symbols is in the editorial section of the news-paper. Distribute one or more newspapers to each group and ask them to find the editorial section and look for cartoons and images.

Step 3: Ask students to pick one cartoon to discuss as a group. Tell them, "Ask one another what the artist is trying to say. How do you know? Have someone in the group read the article that goes with the picture. Does the article make the meaning more clear? What kinds of symbols are used in the picture?"

Step 4: Ask each group to choose a reporter who will write down and present the group's findings.

Reflect

Have students reread what they wrote in their thought journals about symbols, then ask if they still feel the same way or if they feel differently. Ask them again, "Does a visual symbol explain something easier or better than words?"

Follow-up and Extension

Keep a bulletin board space where students can post political cartoons, logos, and other symbols. Challenge other students to explain the imagery.

Applying the Strategy to Curriculum

Divide the week's vocabulary words from social studies, science, or language arts evenly among the class and ask students to make up symbols for their assigned words. Remind them that to be effective the symbol should help other people understand the meaning of the word. Have each student share ideas with the rest of the class, and encourage students to use the symbols to help them study for tests.

Science

1. As a class or in small groups, create symbols for procedures such as measuring, hypothesizing, and estimating. Use the symbols instead of words to give directions for conducting experiments.

2. Teach a unit on the periodic table, focusing on the symbols assigned to each element. Explain why they are necessary (for international standardization), and how they are useful (they provide a unique, shorthand way to refer to long chemical combinations).

Language Arts

1. Have students develop symbols for characters. Remind them that the symbol should reveal something about the character's personality.

2. Have students bring in examples of symbols, either copied down or cut out of a magazine. Then have them put three or more symbols together to create sentences, poems, or stories.

3. As a class, critique why something is or is not a good symbolic representation.

4. Assign students to write captions for symbols or political cartoons.

Math

1. As a class, discuss in what ways math is a symbolic language. Come up with definitions for the symbols (for example, 4, -, and +) that don't use the words *four*, *minus* or *subtract*, or *plus* or *add.* Brainstorm new symbols for mathematical operations.

2. Write out a math operation in words, then discuss as a class which is easier to understand. For example, for the math operation 2 + 2 = 4, write "Take two of something, put it together with two more, then how many do you have?"

3. Develop a classroom secret code using a letter-number match. Use the code to write notes to students, assignments, and so on, and ask them to use the code in similar ways.

4. Assign students to practice writing out word problems and then their symbolic counterparts.

Social Studies

1. As a class, choose an event from the current unit of study and brainstorm a list of the different people or groups involved and what their opinions of the event might have been. Ask students to create a symbol to represent one of the opinions and use it to create a political cartoon. For example, for the Boston Tea Party, the list of groups might be Redcoats, Patriots, tea shippers, American Indians, and European royalty. The Redcoats might draw the Boston Tea Party participants wearing dunce caps or dressed as clowns.

2. Gather symbols from around the world and as a class compare styles, meanings, and uses. Two good sources are *The Symbol Sourcebook* by Harry Dreyfuss and *The Picture Book of Symbols* by Ernest Lehrer.

3. As a class, brainstorm symbols to represent periods in history, famous people, or an opinion on a particular controversy. Symbols for events can be used to create a visual time line; symbols for famous people can be used for headings over a brief written paragraph about the person; symbols for agreeing and dissenting opinions can be used during classroom debates or discussions.

4. Make analysis of political cartoons a regular part of the curriculum. Study symbolic imagery and discuss as a class why the cartoons sometimes communicate opinions more effectively than do words.

5. Teach a unit on Egyptian hieroglyphics or American Indian petroglyphs.

5

Interpersonal Intelligence

Interpersonal intelligence is a critical skill for young people to develop if they are going to be successful personally, socially, and economically in the modern world. As life becomes increasingly fragmented and isolating, especially in large urban areas, meeting people who can become friends becomes less easy a task; highly developed interpersonal abilities can make finding friends easier. In the world of work, increasing use of telecommunication technologies such as the Internet requires employees who can interact comfortably and efficiently with a variety of people. In the Information Age, such a vast range of knowledge and skills is required for success that no one can work successfully in isolation. Teamwork is becoming an increasingly common component of corporate life. Unfortunately, television, computer games, and other isolating technologies have a negative impact on the social skills of today's youth.

This chapter brings interpersonal skills into the classroom by improving students' interdependence, empathy, and communication skills. I recommend that, in addition to the strategies in this chapter, you use cooperative learning strategies whenever feasible and effective. Many school districts have adopted curricula that focus on human interaction, conflict resolution, and self-worth. If your school has yet to add such a program, consider creating a system that rewards, praises, and calls positive attention to teamwork, politeness, and random acts of kindness.

Did You Know?

Studies of elementary classrooms show that 80 percent of talk was teacher talk. If students are to develop verbal skills they must do some of the talking themselves. Group interaction develops language as well as social skills through active listening and participation, interaction, and constant back-and-forth communication (Healy 1990, 96).

Strategy 1

Jigsaw

In Brief

In this strategy, students have responsibility for learning only a portion of an entire lesson and must learn to rely on their classmates to complete the learning puzzle.

Objective

To teach students how to share responsibility for learning

Background

In today's workplace, one individual is seldom solely responsible for a complete project. Generally, people work in teams with selected individuals assigned to various responsibilities.

Lesson 1: Vocabulary Jigsaw

Time

30 minutes (includes 5 minutes prep time)

Preparation

Choose five to twenty vocabulary words from any subject area and write them on the chalkboard.

Focus

Ask students, "What happens when you do not understand the words you read in a story or in a nonfiction work? Do you learn as well as when you do understand them all?"

Teach

Step 1: Divide the class into groups of no more than five students each.

Step 2: Assign each group one to three words, depending on the total number of vocabulary words you gathered. You may assign more if you have few students, but assign no more than five words per group—you want them to be successful with this project. Write the group's name or number next to their assigned words on the chalkboard.

Step 3: Ask students to copy their assigned vocabulary words.

Step 4: Explain that each group is responsible for finding out the definitions of their assigned words. Tell students that you don't want definitions copied from the dictionary; you want them to work together to come up with definitions in their own words. This process allows all group members to share in the process and learn the meaning of all their assigned words.

Step 5: After about fifteen minutes, once every group has learned its assigned words, give each group member a number from one to five (or however many students are in each group). Have students move to new groups by asking all ones to get into a group, all twos, and so on. These new groups will consist of one member from each original group and therefore will have the necessary knowledge to learn the definitions for all the words. The lesson ends when each student's list has every word and its definition.

Step 6: While students are working in small groups, wander the room and compliment groups that are using strong interpersonal skills: staying on task, working together, and helping other group members.

Reflect

Ask students, "How is this method easier or more enjoyable than independent work? In what ways does it work well? When does it not work well?"

Lesson 2: Reading and Comprehension Jigsaw

Time

30 minutes (includes 5 minutes prep time)

Materials

five to eight paragraphs from nonfiction work

Preparation

Photocopy or otherwise mark five to eight paragraphs of nonfiction reading material. Think of three to five questions that you want students to answer about the reading selections. Either write the questions on the chalkboard after step 5, or make photocopies of the questions and pass them out to the class.

Focus

Divide students into groups of no more than five. Explain that during the lesson, each person in each group is solely responsible for some part of the learning. Ask students, "What do you need from your team members for this project to be successful?"

Teach

Step 1: Assign each group of students one or two of the paragraphs that you selected earlier. Either give the groups photocopies, or direct their attention to where in their schoolbooks they can find the paragraphs.

Step 2: Ask groups to read the paragraphs together and take notes on the main ideas and supporting arguments. Explain that they should decide together what is important information, and that each student should keep a copy of the notes as opposed to assigning one recorder or secretary per group.

Step 3: While students work, wander the room and compliment groups that are using strong interpersonal skills: staying on task, working together, and helping one another.

Step 4: After about ten minutes, once every group has read and discussed its assigned paragraphs, give each group member a number from one to five (or however many students are in each group). Have students move to new groups by asking all ones to form a group, all twos, and so on. These new groups will consist of one member from each original group, and therefore will have the necessary knowledge to understand all of the paragraphs.

Step 5: Allow the new groups about ten minutes to share their information (let them use their notes), then write on the chalkboard the questions you prepared earlier and assign the groups to answer them independently in writing.

Reflect

Ask students, "How many felt confident about your answers to the questions? What was it like to trust the information provided by other group members?"

Lesson 3: Research Jigsaw

Time

45 to 55 minutes (includes 10 to 20 minutes prep time)

Materials

encyclopedias (if you have no encyclopedias, photocopy appropriate pages from encyclopedias)

textbooks

Preparation

Write five to six research questions about a current study topic or an upcoming study unit, such as "What are the parts of a cell?" "How do cells pass information?" "What does a chromosome do?"

Focus

Divide students into groups of no more than five. Explain that during the lesson, each person in each group is solely responsible for only one part of the entire learning task. Ask students, "What do you need from your team members for this exercise to be successful? When you have difficulty with your part of the assignment, what can you do?" (Ask for help from your team.)

Teach

Step 1: Give each group of students one research question.

Step 2: Explain to the class that each group must find the answers to its assigned questions, and that the group must use more than one source to find the answer. As a class, briefly discuss the kinds of places they can look: textbooks, encyclopedia, library books, and so on. Ask them to work together to find and discuss information and to learn the answer to the research question. Each member of the group will share with the next group what was learned. Suggest that note taking and sketches will help.

Step 3: While students are working, wander the room and compliment groups that are using strong interpersonal skills: staying on task, working together, and helping other group members.

Step 4: After about fifteen minutes, once every group has found answers for its assigned research question, assign each group member a number from one to five or however many students are in each group. Have students move to new groups by asking all ones to form a group, all twos, and so on. These new groups will consist of one member from each original group, and therefore will have the necessary knowledge to answer all research questions.

Step 5: After fifteen minutes for sharing, bring the class together and, as one group, go over the answers to the research questions.

Reflect

Ask students, "How did it go when you shared information in your second group? Did other group members learn and understand your information? Did you understand their information? Why or why not?"

Follow-up and Extension

Try a homework jigsaw. Send students home with one part of a research or vocabulary assignment. Allow time the next morning for groups to share information.

Applying the Strategy to Curriculum

Note: All applications use the first group–second group structure of the jigsaw strategy.

1. Divide reading assignments. The first groups each learn one passage and take notes on the main idea and supporting arguments. The second groups share information from all passages.
2. Divide vocabulary words among groups. The second groups learn and review all the words.
3. Each group makes up a rap or song to remember facts about a current study unit. The second groups learn all the songs.

Science

Have the first groups research one scientist or one invention. The second groups learn about all five scientists or inventions.

Language Arts

1. Assign the first groups one character each from a current reading. Ask them to evaluate the character's personality. The second group will discuss and take notes on the personalities of all characters.

2. Assign first groups one reading passage in a consecutive series of reading passages to practice aloud. Ask students in second groups to figure out in what order the passages go. Then they can perform the whole series in order.

3. Assign first groups one role in a play and have students practice reading aloud their roles. Once students are in the second group, they can perform the whole play.

4. Have each first group practice reciting different stanzas of a poem. When the second groups come together they will learn and perform the entire poem.

5. Have each group write one scene of a play or one part of a story. When the second groups come together they will have a whole story.

Math

Each group is responsible for creating one word problem and working out the solution. Second groups work on finding the right answers to the different problems.

Social Studies

1. Assign different but related research questions to each first group (for example, famous people, inventions that changed the world, colonies in early America, cultures from various American Indian tribes). When the second groups meet and share their information, every student will have a well-rounded idea of the topic.

2. Assign each first group to learn either a skill, a game, a craft, a song, or a story. In the second groups, each student is responsible for teaching the group what he or she learned.

3. First groups learn about one aspect of a culture: for example, clothing, food, traditions, language, or environment. Second groups share all the information.

Physical Education

First groups practice one skill associated with a particular game or sport (kicking into a goal, dribbling, passing, and so on). Each student in the second groups is responsible for teaching the skill he or she just learned to other group members.

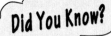

Did You Know?

Winston Churchill once said, "I am always ready to learn, but I do not always like being taught."

Strategy 2

Brainstorming

In Brief

These lessons teach students the rules, objectives, and benefits of group brainstorming.

Objective

To teach students to use brainstorming to increase their creative thinking skills: originality, fluency, flexibility, and elaboration

Background

Brainstorming is an increasingly common technique in the business world, where it is used to boost ideas and creativity. It follows the premise that many brains are better than one.

Lesson 1: Brainstorming for Fluency and Originality

Time

22 minutes (includes 2 minutes prep time)

Materials

one for each group of a large sheet of newsprint or butcher paper

markers, crayons, or pencils (markers and crayons are more colorful and enjoyable)

Preparation

Divide the class into groups of no more than four. Give each group a piece of newsprint or butcher paper, and give each student a crayon or marker.

Focus

Ask students, "Has anyone ever noticed how one idea can lead to another idea? Why do you think that happens? Can anyone give me an example?" Explain that the class is going to learn how to brainstorm, which is a way to develop ideas by working together. Tell them, "Before we start I want to go over a few ground rules for brainstorming. For us to be most creative, we have to feel as though we won't get teased or put down because of our ideas. Does anyone have any ideas about how we can stop that from happening?" Write students' ideas on the chalkboard. Explain that brainstorming works because sometimes someone says a wild or crazy idea that isn't realistic, but it gives someone else a good idea that is possible to do. Ask students, "What do you think would happen if we didn't allow people to say their crazy ideas out loud?" Explain that the success of brainstorming depends on everyone's participation. Ask students, "How can we be sure that everyone will participate?" Write students' ideas on the board.

Teach

Step 1: Ask one student in each group to write the following main topic in the middle of the page and circle it: A New Kind of Transportation.

Step 2: Explain that you are going to ask a question and you want the student groups to say their ideas about that question out loud so that other group members can get more ideas. They will write the ideas around the main topic. Remind them to keep the paper in the middle of the table so everyone can be writing while they talk about their ideas. Also remind the groups to occasionally turn the paper around so everyone can see what other members of the group are writing.

Step 3: Tell them, "Okay, start brainstorming about this question: 'How can we change or improve the ways we get from place to place?'"

Step 4: Allow seven to ten minutes for writing and discussion. Compliment the groups that are working well together and praise involvement and discussion.

REMINDER

Praise is important during a brainstorming session, but try not to praise particular ideas. Students may then feel intimidated to share ideas for fear of being judged.

Step 5: After the brainstorming session, bring the class together and ask each group to share ideas while you write them on the chalkboard.

Step 6: As a class, discuss which ideas are original. Explain that *original* means "one of a kind," or that other groups didn't think of it. Put asterisks next to those ideas.

Reflect

Ask students, "Now that you've tried brainstorming, how is thinking up ideas together different from thinking up ideas alone?"

Lesson 2: Brainstorming for Flexibility and Elaboration

Time

25 minutes (includes 5 minutes prep time)

Materials

one copy for each student of the Elaboration work sheet

Preparation

Make copies of Elaboration work sheet.

Focus

Ask students, "Has anyone ever noticed how changing one part of a story or event can cause lots of other changes?" Ask students to volunteer examples, then ask, "How would 'The Three Little Pigs' change if the first pig built his house out of bricks, or if the wolf accepted *no* for an answer?"

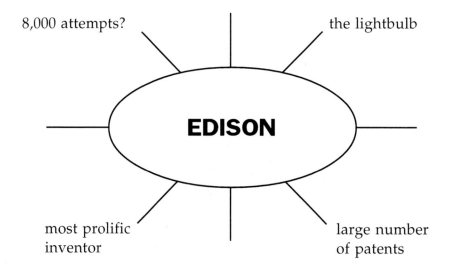

Teach

Step 1: Ask a student to name one literary or historical figure who appears in class material.

Step 2: As a class, brainstorm things you know about that person's life—personality, associated events, crises, friends, enemies, and so on—from the reading. Write all ideas on the chalkboard.

Step 3: Pass out Elaboration work sheets. Ask students to write the name of the character or famous person in the topic blank.

Step 4: Ask students to pick one fact from the list on the board. Tell them that in order to fill out the work sheet, they will have to imagine that fact has changed. If Wilbur from *Charlotte's Web* is your character, you might change the fact that he is a pig or you might change the fact that he and Charlotte are friends.

Step 5: Direct students to write the change into one of the numbered boxes on the work sheet.

Step 6: In the other three boxes, students should write their ideas about how the story or events might turn out differently because of the change in the box.

Step 7: Ask some students to share their ideas with the class.

Step 8: Ask students to brainstorm some other possible changes. Write their ideas on the board.

Step 9: In box 2, students should select a different change from the first box by using ideas on the board or they can use ideas of their own. They should reflect in the three connected boxes how things might turn out differently.

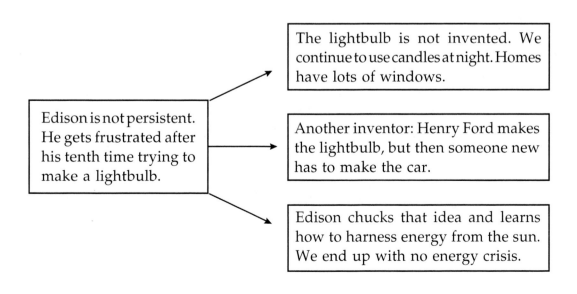

Strategy 2 Work Sheet

Elaboration

Name: _____

Topic: _____

What happens differently? How would that change affect the rest of the story?

1.

2.

Reflect

Ask students, "Did listening to your classmates' ideas help you come up with more ideas of your own? How?"

Follow-up and Extension

Use class brainstorming sessions to come up with ideas for field trips, special celebration days, party ideas, and a class reward system. Use Elaboration work sheets to discuss conflict resolution skills.

Applying the Strategy to Curriculum

1. On the first day of a new unit, introduce the subject matter, then have a class brainstorming session to come up with questions to answer during the course of the unit.

2. Before assigning students to write a story, poem, report, or essay for any subject, have them brainstorm ideas in small groups.

Science

1. Ask students to imagine that some fundamental rules of science (gravity, energy, and so on) have changed. Follow the steps in lesson 2 to brainstorm how the changes would affect life for plants, humans and other animals.

2. Before assigning students to write reports on inventions or discoveries, have them complete Elaboration work sheets to brainstorm answers to the question "What if this invention or discovery had never been made?"

3. Have students brainstorm in small groups about a science topic such as outer space, then share the results as a class and note and acknowledge original ideas.

Language Arts

1. Pick a topic about language arts, such as a funny character or a sad setting and have students brainstorm ideas in small groups. Share the results as a class and note some original ideas.

2. Follow the steps in lesson 2 to change part of a story and brainstorm how that change affects the rest of the story. As a variation on this exercise, begin by brainstorming as a class which parts of a story could change, then assign students to pick two aspects with which to complete an Elaboration work sheet.

Social Studies

1. As a class, brainstorm things that could have happened to change the course of a particular historic event. Have students complete an Elaboration work sheet about two of the possible changes, then

ask them to use the information in their charts to rewrite the event as a "what if" story.

2. As a class, brainstorm all possible opinions on a historic, political, or cultural topic.

Physical Education

1. Brainstorm new rules for a game.

2. As a class, discuss how new rules might change how the game is played.

Strategy 3

Talk, Listen, and Pass the Bag

In Brief

Students use a beanbag-passing game to practice the skills of conversation: listening and speaking. Whoever has the bag does the talking, and the one to get the bag must repeat what she heard from the previous holder before getting to share her ideas.

Time

35 to 40 minutes (includes 10 minutes prep time)

Objective

To teach students how to take part in a conversation by voicing their opinions clearly, and by listening and rephrasing the opinions of others

Background

I have heard it said that a conversation is like a quick game of catch. No one should hold onto the ball too long and everyone should be paying attention. When you work with elementary children it becomes apparent that the ability to listen actively to others and to state clearly your opinions are valuable skills that are currently underdeveloped in our young people.

Lesson 1: Beanbag Pulpit

Materials

six or seven small beanbags or Hacky-Sacks (handmade or bought)

Preparation

Select a current topic from any unit of study that lends itself to opinion, or else a current topic of contention in the classroom or school. For example, "Who is the smartest character in the story we are reading?" "Should gum be allowed in school?" "Are good manners important?" or "What twentieth century invention has most changed our lives?" Gather six or seven beanbags or make your own by filling odd socks with beans and tying them in knots.

Focus

Ask students, "How do you know when someone is really listening to you? What are the body signals? Does it feel good to be really listened to?" Tell them, "The art of good conversation is difficult because it requires two important and hard-to-learn skills: listening and speaking with clarity." Ask students, "Who would like to learn to become a good listener and speaker? Who would like to play catch? Who would like to do both at once?"

Teach

Step 1: Put students in groups of four to six. Seat them facing one another in a circle or around desks or tables. Review with the class the question you selected from your current curriculum or school concerns.

Step 2: Explain that each group will be given a beanbag. The person holding the beanbag is the talker and everyone else must listen. Each person in the group should have a chance to hold the beanbag before the end of the activity.

Step 3: The talker holds the bag and voices his opinion as clearly and completely as possible.

> Students' opinions should give reasons: "I believe this because . . ."
>
> REMINDER

Step 4: The speaker then passes the bag to anyone else in the group who has not spoken.

Step 5: The next speaker rephrases or retells what the person before him thinks before going on to voice his opinion.

Step 6: Wander the room and listen to the conversations closely. Pay attention to the language and listening skills so you will know what kinds of suggestions to make the next time you try this activity.

Reflect

Ask a few students to share what the experience was like for them. Have the class write in their thought journals one opinion voiced by someone else in their group.

Follow-up and Extension

Once students have become adept at speaking and listening during the beanbag pulpit activity, make a transition to allow for more fluid conversation. Have students talk in turn and allow other students to signal (raise their hands or some other appropriate indication) when they want the bag. Teach them such transition phrases as, "What I heard you say was . . . and what I think is . . . "

Applying the Strategy to Curriculum

Science

1. Have students discuss the most interesting inventor or the least likely invention to be useable in ten years.
2. Have students evaluate the money spent on the space program: Should the United States spend more? Less? Why or why not?

Language Arts

1. Look for chances to voice opinions about the literature you are reading. Is the character about to make an important decision? Can students debate what she should do? What about a decision that has already been made? Was there a better decision? Would it have made sense for the character to make a different decision? What about the setting? Could that be changed? What would make a better setting and why?
2. As a precursor to a book report, have students discuss their favorite book.

Social Studies

1. Discuss favorite American Indian tribes or favorite explorers, places students would most like to live if they were transported to the time of the current history unit.
2. Discuss current events. Have students bring in opinion columns from the local newspaper to gather a grab-bag of potential beanbag pulpit topics.

3. Let students pick a hot topic to discuss. Have them write opinion papers once they finish the beanbag pulpit exercise.

Math

Have the talker create a word problem and the next person solve the problem before creating her own.

Did You Know?

I discussed with my students the book *Emotional Intelligence* and how it revealed that group interaction skills were more important to success than IQ, even in the science fields. A few students were skeptical until we took a field trip to Jet Propulsion Laboratories. My students excitedly pointed out to me how all the engineers and rocket scientists were gathered together and working in groups around the space equipment and materials.

Strategy 4

Five Different Identities

In Brief

In lesson 1 students act out reactions to situations as if they were one of a cast of characters. In lesson 2, they work together to decide how a specific character or person might respond to a given situation.

Objectives

To teach students how to predict a person's opinions and responses based on personality

To teach students to use predictions to deepen understanding of the person or the subject matter

Background

Fiction writers often imagine their characters in situations that have nothing to do with the story they are writing to gain a greater understanding of the characters' motivations and personalities. When we know people well, we can sometimes predict their opinions and responses to specific situations.

Lesson 1: Five Identities, Five Opinions, Five Responses

(adapted from Lazear 1991a)

Time

35 minutes (includes 5 minutes prep time)

Materials

twenty-five index cards

Preparation

Write each of the following identities on five index cards for a total of twenty-five cards: principal, teacher, two-year-old, painter, custodian.

Focus

Ask students, "If there were a fire, how might a fearful person respond? What about a stubborn person? A brave person? Why do different people respond differently to the same situation?"

Teach

Step 1: Organize students into groups of four or five.

Step 2: Give each group one set of index cards and have each student take one card. Explain to students that they are going to play a guessing game by pretending they are the persons on their cards.

Step 3: Read the following description to your class: "Ten cans of different colors of paint are lying open on the floor in the middle of the school's multipurpose room. Brushes and rollers are leaning on the wall nearby. Many people use the room throughout the day."

Step 4: After reading the situation, have students describe to their group their feelings and reactions to the situation you just read as if they were the persons on their cards. Group members should try to guess one another's identity based on the feelings students describe.

Reflect

Come together as a class and discuss why the different identities had different reactions to the same situation. Ask students, "What is it like to guess how other people would think and respond?"

Lesson 2: Predict the Response

Time

35 minutes (includes 5 minutes prep time)

Materials

one copy for each student of Pretend Situation handout

Preparation

Choose a literary character, famous person, or type of person (for example, a slave trader or an immigrant from China) from any current lesson.

Focus

Ask students, "Do you ever argue? How do you act when you are in an argument? Do different people act differently when they argue?"

Teach

Step 1: Explain to students that they are going to play a guessing game to imagine what the reaction of a historical or literary character might be to a particular situation.

Step 2: Ask for a student volunteer to read aloud the first situation on the handout. Ask the class if the situation calls for a response or an opinion. (The first situation requires a response; the second, a response or an opinion; the third, a response; the fourth, a response or an opinion; the fifth, a response; the sixth, a response or an opinion; and the seventh, an opinion.)

Step 3: Brainstorm all possible responses to or opinions about the situation. Then decide which of the responses or opinions best fits the historical or literary character.

Step 4: Divide the class into groups of about four students each for situation 2. Assign each group a different character to think about. Allow about five minutes for brainstorming, then ask for a volunteer from each group to perform as if she were that character.

Imagine you are the person on the card. How do you think or feel about the following situations? What would you do?

1. My kitten has wandered out onto a high wall. It is very windy and the wall is two hundred feet above the ground. I can reach the kitten either by crawling through a window that is at one end of the wall (the kitten is at the other) or by climbing an old, wobbly ladder.

2. A young person who has difficulty walking because she has hurt her foot trips and falls in the cafeteria. Her milk and food spills and everyone around her is laughing. She is very embarrassed and does not want to get up.

3. I've signed up for a go-cart race, but my go-cart was stolen. The race is in two days.

4. The neighborhood I live in is in turmoil. Neighbors are not getting along. Some are playing mean pranks on people they don't like. Some are not speaking to anyone. A few are trying to sell their homes and move out. Many are being very inconsiderate about where they park their cars and how clean they keep their yards. Some have even been lighting fires in trash cans. I have been asked to speak at a neighborhood meeting.

5. I see an unmarked container with strange and interesting green goop dripping from it sitting in the middle of the street.

6. An expensive diamond has been stolen from a jewelry store. I was in the store at the time of the theft. Someone I know didn't steal the diamond has been accused and arrested.

7. Congress has decided to shut down the public school system. From now on, families must pay for school or keep their kids at home.

Reflect

Ask students, "Is it easy or difficult to imagine what another person might say or do? Why?"

Follow-up and Extension

Keep five identity index cards on hand. When the class has a few extra minutes before recess, make up a funny, sad, or tense situation and have students act out the identity responses for the various identities. When a class conflict arises, use the five identity cards to brainstorm various good and bad responses and solutions.

Applying the Strategy to Curriculum

1. When students are frustrated or struggling with a new skill, ask them to imagine they are one of the identities on the list on the Identities work sheet. Ask them to think about what that person would do to solve the problem, learn the skill, or find the answer.

2. Reteach lesson 1, using situations and conflicts from current lesson plans. Choose identities from the Identities work sheet that will work within the particular situation. For example, have a farmer, an animal, a child, a restaurant owner, and a vegetarian respond to the idea of *Charlotte's Web*'s Wilbur becoming food. Or have a slave owner, a slave, a farmer in the North, a Quaker, and an American Indian respond to the idea of ending slavery.

Science

1. Write the names of famous inventors and scientists on index cards. Repeat the steps in lesson 1 and ask students to imagine the inventors' opinions about modern inventions or their advice about solving a problem or overcoming a difficulty. Asking students to perform in front of the class is an option.

2. Assign students to write a dialog in which a famous scientist gives advice to a character in the current language arts reading.

Language Arts

1. Write the major and perhaps minor characters onto individual index cards. Put the characters in various dilemmas and situations and decide how they might act.

2. Take a situation that the main character in your reading is going through. Pick five characters from the Identities work sheet and try to guess how they might handle the same situation.

3. When a class conflict arises, work as a class to imagine how characters from the current reading might resolve the conflict or what their opinions of the situation might be.

Strategy 4 Work Sheet   Identities

Name: _____

Add identities to the list as you read and learn about other characters or kinds of people.

African American	judge
American Indian (or particular tribe member)	lawyer
	Mexican American
architect	Minuteman
artist	mom
Asian American	movie star
athlete	musician
baby	optimist
blacksmith	Patriot
Canadian	pessimist
construction worker	pioneer
dad	plantation owner
doctor	police officer
engineer	Puritan
explorer	Quaker
farmer	railroad engineer
firefighter	Redcoat
free person	restaurant owner
French person	rock-and-roll star
gold miner	sharecropper
grandfather	shipper
grandmother	singer
hairdresser	slave
housekeeper	store owner
immigrant (perhaps from a specific country)	teacher
	teenager
innkeeper	trapper
insurance salesperson	truck driver
journalist	

Social Studies

1. Write the names of famous people the class is studying onto individual index cards. As the class learns more about some of the people's character traits, direct students to add notes to the cards. As a class activity, imagine the historical figures in various situations to see how they might respond.

2. Have students give persuasive speeches as if they were characters from history examining a current situation.

3. Assign students to write a dialog in which one identity gives advice to another identity about a historical conflict.

4. Have students write reports from the perspective of particular historical figures explaining why they participated in a particular historical event.

Strategy 5

The Most Important Thing

In Brief

Students each pick a main point from a unit of study just completed. All students share their ideas for the main point, learning from the others' ideas of what was most important. The final list of powerful, important, and surprising points will also let you know which parts of the unit most excited and stimulated students.

Time

10 minutes

Objective

To encourage students to summarize what they've learned

Background

Students who are able to summarize what they've learned are likely to retain more of the concepts and information they encounter. In addition, when students compare their own summaries to those of other students, they learn that different parts of the lesson are important to different learners.

Lesson 1: The Most Important Thing

You can use this strategy in conjunction with any lesson, field trip, guest presentation, film, or other learning experience. It is especially helpful following a lesson on a complex subject with a number of ideas and topics; for example, immigration, the Constitution, or the use of irony in writing.

Teach

Step 1: Divide the class into groups of four or five students. Give each group one piece of writing paper and ask them to write down each group member's answer to this question: "What is the most interesting (surprising, powerful, intriguing) thing you learned?"

Step 2: After about five minutes, call the class together and ask the students to share their answers. Write their responses on the chalkboard or overhead projector. As you progress around the classroom, students may begin to repeat one another. If a response is already on the board, put a check mark next to it. Some answers will have many check marks, some will have none.

Reflect

Ask students, "Why do you think we all have such different ideas about what was most interesting, powerful, or surprising?" You want students to recognize that, as different individuals, they have different values and opinions.

Strategy 6

The Interdependent Duet

In Brief

This strategy divides the class into two groups, one of which learn a lesson with you while the other remain in their seats. The "expert" half of the class will then teach the lesson to the students who did not hear the lesson from you. Partners will reverse roles for different lessons, creating an interdependence among partners.

Objectives

To teach students to work as a team and depend upon one another

To help students learn by teaching others

Background

It is often said that we learn 10 percent of what we hear, 30 percent of what we see, and 80 percent of what we do. Add to this truism that we learn 99 percent of what we teach. When students teach others what they know, they cement their knowledge of the material while they learn to work as a team.

Lesson 1: The Craft of Teaching

Time

30 minutes

Focus

Ask students, "How do you feel when you are trying to learn something new and someone is rushing you?"

Teach

Step 1: Ask students to work in groups of about four to discuss and answer the following questions, one at a time, stopping to share between questions (see step 2). Write the questions on the chalkboard as you ask them.

- What words does a teacher use to encourage you? What words discourage you from learning?

- What is the most important thing that helps you when you are frustrated and cannot learn something? Time? Understanding? A new way of teaching? Something else?

- What happens if a teacher does not know the information he is teaching?

Step 2: Allow about three minutes for each question. Ask each group to share its responses with the rest of the class before moving on to the next question.

Reflect

Ask students to answer the following question in their thought journals: "If you were a teacher, what would you do if a student was not able to learn what you were teaching?"

Lesson 2: An Interdependent Duet

Time

30 minutes

Preparation

Prepare two relatively simple lesson plans in any subject. Prepare independent seat work for students not working with you.

Focus

Ask students, "When do you like to work with a partner? When is it frustrating?" Discuss students' responses and write them on the chalkboard.

Teach

Step 1: Divide the class into pairs (if you have an odd number of students, create one threesome).

Step 2: Explain that you are going to teach a lesson to one-half the class. Bring students up in small groups without their partners, who should be provided with interesting seat work so they don't feel left out.

Step 3: Teach one basic lesson in any subject area, working with a small, obtainable objective (for example, how a suffix changes the meaning of a root or how to flip the second fraction when dividing).

Step 4: When you feel confident that the students understand, ask them to teach the lesson to their partners.

Step 5: Repeat the strategy on the following day by teaching the second half of the class a new lesson and having them teach their partners.

Reflect

Ask students to answer the following questions in their thought journals: "How does it feel to teach? To learn from another student?"

Follow-up and Extension

Use interdependent duets to teach new students the classroom rules and school procedures.

Applying the Strategy to Curriculum

Science

Give half the class step-by-step instructions for how to carry out an experiment. Tell them they cannot touch the equipment themselves, but they can explain the steps to their partners. Switch roles on the next experiment.

Language Arts

1. Teach one group how to address a letter.
2. Teach one group how to address a party invitation.
3. Teach one group a few spelling tricks.
4. Teach one group how to recite a poem or sing a song. After they have taught their partners, ask for volunteers to perform.

Math

Choose five students to become experts on particular math skills. Train an expert in adding fractions, an expert in subtracting, an expert in using fraction pies, an expert in multiplying fractions, and an expert in division. Ask them to teach the rest of the class in small groups of four to five students at a time.

Social Studies

1. Teach half the students about early tools.
2. Explain the reason behind an amendment to the Constitution. The next day, give the partners a different amendment.
3. Teach one-third of your students about the middle colonies, one-third about the New England colonies, and one-third about the southern colonies. Arrange the class in threesomes to teach one another.

Physical Education

Choose five students to become experts on a specific step or skill. For instance, teach one how to dribble a ball, one how to make a goal, one how to block a goal, and two others how to pass with their feet. Have the experts teach their skills to other students.

6

Intrapersonal Intelligence

Intrapersonal intelligence, like interpersonal intelligence, is a crucial component of success in today's world. The ability to understand oneself, the willpower to control one's impulses, and the instincts of good guessing are all useful skills that can pave the way to social and economic rewards.

This chapter outlines four easy strategies that incorporate intrapersonal skills into the general curriculum by activating inner talk: wondering, thinking intuitively, making connections, and drawing conclusions. Beyond these strategies, intrapersonal skills are used in the classroom every time you provide time for your students to engage in reflection. Reflect upon feelings, thoughts, responses, successes, and failures. Reflect through writing, body language, drawing, or music. Reflection helps students understand their own motivations, interests, and learning styles. It is a recipe for self-awareness.

Did You Know?

In *Endangered Minds*, Jane Healy (1990) writes: "Human brains are not only capable of acquiring knowledge; they also hold the potential for wisdom. But wisdom has its own curriculum: conversation, thought, imagination, empathy, reflection. Youths who lack these basics, who cannot ponder what they have learned, are poorly equipped to become managers of the human enterprise in any era" (346).

Strategy 1

Promoting Wonder

In Brief

These three lessons encourage students to ask increasingly complex and original questions about material, which in turn excites further interest in the subject.

Objective

To encourage students to develop active rather than passive learning styles

Background

Before the age of two, children start to turn their wondering into words: "How come...?" "Why...?" But by the time most people reach school age, they are taught to decrease questioning and increase listening. Most school curricula have set agendas with little time to wander off into independent inquiry. This strategy seeks to ignite students' desire to ask questions, an activity that so often leads to creative discovery and invention.

Lesson 1: A Big, Fat, Juicy Question

Time

20 minutes

Materials

thought journals

Focus

Ask students what kind of food they would describe as good, fat, and juicy. Ask them, "Is it nutritious? Does it make your mouth water just thinking about it?" Say that you think questions can be like that, too. Some questions are okay questions; they're pretty good. But other questions are good, fat, juicy questions. Ask students, "In what way can we say that a juicy question is also a nutritious or healthy question?" Allow students to come up with their own reasons.

Teach

Step 1:   On the chalkboard or overhead projector make two columns. Title one column "Juicy" and the other column "Not Juicy."

Step 2: Read aloud the following questions, and have students vote on whether each is juicy or not juicy. Based on their decisions, write the questions in the appropriate column.

- Where were you born? (not juicy)

- If you were born in a different place and raised in a different family, how would you be different? (juicy)

- Who is in your family? (not juicy)

- Where do you live? (not juicy)

- What is your ideal kind of place to live? (juicy)

- Can you name a few of your friends? (not juicy)

- What is a good friend like? (juicy)

- What is a juicy question? (not juicy)

- How is a juicy question more nutritious? (juicy)

Step 3: Ask students to answer the last two questions. Bring them to the understanding that a juicy question requires more thought to answer. If they can answer the question easily, off the tops of their heads, or even quickly by looking in a resource book, it is not juicy. If the question can be answered in a variety of ways, depending on which answer works best for the person answering the question, then it is a juicy question.

Step 4: Ask students to write the "Juicy" and "Not Juicy" headings in their thought journals.

Step 5: As a class, brainstorm juicy and not-juicy questions about any subject you are presently studying (science and social studies work particularly well; language arts and math questions can be complex). Following are some examples: What brought settlers to the West? (juicy) When did the gold rush begin? (not juicy) How is a living organism similar to a city? (juicy) What are the main components of a cell? (not juicy)

Step 6: Students will realize that some questions fall into both categories. As a class, discuss why. A statement that starts with *describe*, for example, can be answered briefly and without thought, or in detail with much thought. The response to "Describe the city" can have a not-juicy answer, such as "It has lots of buildings," and a juicy answer, such as "It drips with humidity like a faucet that lost its washer."

Reflect

Ask students, "A juicy question can make your mouth water. What does that mean?" Allow students to respond with their own ideas.

Lesson 2: Before, During, and After

Time

5 to 10 minutes

Materials

thought journals

folders with pockets

bulletin board

photographs, drawings, poems, and newspaper and magazine articles about a lesson in any curriculum area

Preparation

Gather materials to introduce the chosen topic. At least a week before beginning a new unit, give students a preview of what they will be studying: tell them some of the vocabulary words, show them pictures, bring in a poem or news article. Ask them to write in their thought journals three to five questions they have about the subject based on the preview you've given them. At the end of the day, collect their journals and start a display by posting some of the questions on a bulletin board (write each on a separate piece of paper with the student's name under it) along with the materials you brought in to introduce them to the unit. Ask students to spend time before and during the unit collecting things—pictures, news articles, thoughts from their parents, more questions they think of, and so on—about the subject.

For example, suppose that you are starting a unit on the planets. Tell students the names of some of the planets. Ask them to write down some questions they have about those planets. Find and read a story or a poem about the planets. Share with the class a news article on current space technology. Ask them to talk to their parents and look for pictures and articles about the planets.

As soon as you start teaching the unit, ask students to turn in the items they have been collecting. Add their materials to the bulletin board or other display area. Compliment students who are bringing in items and share their discoveries with the rest of the class. Provide class time for everyone to explore the display area, and make sure that students understand that the display will be up and changing throughout the lesson. Periodically, ask students to refer to the questions in their thought journals. Are any of the questions getting answered? Do they have new questions? Are their new questions different from their first questions? In what ways? Be sure to discuss their new questions. Discuss with the students how their questions are changing as they learn more. Questions usually become more directed, for example, from "What are the planets' names?" to "Why do planets have varying temperatures?" Ask students to hypothesize why the questions change as they learn more.

When the unit is complete, review the bulletin board questions as a class. Find out which questions were answered and which were not answered. Ask students if they have any new questions. Discuss ways students can find answers to some of the questions that were not answered in the unit. Encourage students to share any answers they find by bringing in information to share.

Reflect

Ask students why they think you wanted them to ask questions that weren't going to be answered in the unit. Encourage such answers as, "You wanted us to spark an interest in planets." "You hoped we'd get excited." "By being curious we would learn more."

Lesson 3: Rewarding the Question

Time

varies

Materials

bulletin board

Preparation

Create a Juicy Question of the Week poster. Create a Juicy Question Certificate of Merit and make copies.

Teach

You can regularly use the following methods in the classroom to encourage students to engage in active wondering, pondering, and questioning.

- Allow an extended question-and-answer period after every lesson.
- Model the act of wondering for your students. You can start questions with the phrase, "What I am wondering is . . . " When you ask students questions, say, "What do you wonder about . . . ?"

- Don't be embarrassed if you can't answer a question. Students often love to find answers to questions their teachers can't answer. I usually say, "Boy, that's a good question! I'm stumped! I wonder where we might find the answer!"

- When a student asks a juicy question, write it in big letters with the student's name beneath and post it on the wall. Scatter students' juicy questions around the classroom.

- Create a Juicy Question of the Week poster with space for the question, the name of the student who asked it, and maybe even a place for a photo!

- Develop a Juicy Question Certificate of Merit to hand out when a student asks a juicy question.

- If your class has a student of the week, have the rest of the class conduct an interview. Reward those students who ask good, juicy questions.

Follow-up and Extension

Prepare for a guest speaker or field trip by reteaching this lesson. Prepare a list of juicy questions to ask during the field trip or during the speaker's presentation. Post a list of Questions the Teacher Is Pondering, so students know you wonder about things, too. Encourage parents to keep question journals in which they note questions their children ask; suggest that students bring the journals on visits to the public library.

Applying the Strategy to Curriculum

1. Carry out the lesson with any unit of study.

2. On tests, give students credit for coming up with a good, juicy question about the subject matter.

3. As a class, brainstorm good, juicy questions on a subject; ask each student to pick one question to answer in a report or project.

4. Post students' juicy questions on a bulletin board or in a display area.

Language Arts

1. Encourage students to write down and ask questions about subjects alluded to or directly discussed in reading materials. Do they have questions about the lead character's job as a biologist or about the story's setting, New Orleans? Give students attention and recognition for their pondering (post their questions, praise their pondering, ask them to add the question to the growing list, and so on).

2. Ask students to guess the plot or central tension of a story after they have read only the first page or paragraph.

3. Brainstorm questions about a particular subject. Have students pick one or two questions and write a report (must be a very juicy question), a paragraph, or a letter that answers the questions they chose.

4. Have students write a riddle poem. See the following example.

> I move leaves without touch.
>
> I send shivers across water.
>
> Who am I?
>
> I am the Wind.

Math

1. Assign students to write down math problems that they have encountered in everyday life, for example, how much wood does it take to build a tree house, how high is a wall, and so on.

2. Assign a problem that can be solved in a variety of ways (for example, measure a snowflake). Have students ponder possible ways to solve the problem. Then have students create similar math problems.

Social Studies

Assign students to write riddle poems about famous people.

Strategy 2

Look Before You Leap

In Brief

These two lessons, while very different from each other, are designed to stretch students' thinking. In lesson 1, students make musical associations with their topic; in lesson 2, they build a personal inventory of what they know and what they want to know about a topic.

Objectives

To encourage students to use intuition and association before embarking on a learning experience

To help students think in new ways about information they already know

Background

Intuitive guessing and the ability to associate unrelated ideas are two central intrapersonal skills.

Lesson 1: Making Connections

Time

25 to 35 minutes (includes 10 to 20 minutes prep time)

Materials

CD or cassette player

music tapes or CDs (suggestions: Mozart's Concerto 27 in B-flat Major, Andreas Vollenweider's *White Winds*, Andrew Lloyd Weber's *Phantom of the Opera,* instrumental reggae)

Preparation

Pick out three diverse pieces of music to play. Set up the player and the music.

Focus

Ask students, "What kinds of music do we hear when we are watching a mystery movie? How about a comedy?" Engage the class in a discussion about how different kinds of music are often associated with different kinds of events or feelings.

Teach

Note: You may use this lesson with any unit. Throughout the lesson, fill in the blanks with whatever unit you think will work well with this exercise.

Step 1: Remind the class of the topic. Briefly review the main concepts, characters, vocabulary, and so on.

Step 2: Tell students, "We are going to spend time today thinking about_____in a different way from the way we usually think about it. We are going to listen to music and pretend that the music we hear is the musical score for a movie about _____."

Step 3: Explain that you will play each piece of music for three minutes, during which time you want students to concentrate and imagine they are watching a movie about the topic.

Step 4: When the three minutes are up, ask students, "What did you imagine was happening in the movie while you listened to the music? Did anyone get ideas about what the movie was telling us about _____?" Discuss students' answers as a class. If the music is dramatic, students might talk about seeing images of the explorers crossing the ocean or first sighting land. Or they might imagine the movie is about how cells grow and work together, or about the conflicts between the colonists and the American Indians.

Step 5:   Go through the activity twice more using two different kinds of music.

Reflect

Ask students, "Do you think differently about _____?" "How did the music affect what you thought about?" "Which music matched our topic the best? Why do you think so?" Ask students, "Could we do this same activity with art or dance? How would it work?" As a follow-up, act out some of the students' suggestions.

Lesson 2: KWG Charts

(adapted from Ogle 1986)

Time

15 minutes

Materials

thought journals

Focus

Ask students, "Does anyone remember why we should stop and think about a subject before we begin to study it?" Allow a few minutes for class discussion.

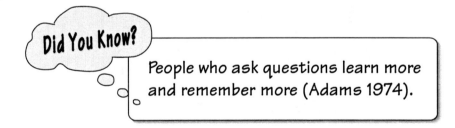

Did You Know?

People who ask questions learn more and remember more (Adams 1974).

Teach

Step 1:   Ask students to make three columns on a page in their thought journals while you demonstrate on the chalkboard.

Step 2:   Label the first column *K* for know, the second *W* for wonder, and the third *G* for guess.

Step 3: Let the class know what the next unit of study is. Discuss as a class some things you already know about the topic. Ask students to write each fact they know in the K column while you demonstrate with the columns on the chalkboard. For instance, students might already know the name of one explorer, or they may know that cells are a part of their bodies, and so forth.

Step 4: Allow students some time to work independently, writing down other things they know.

Step 5: Ask students to list what they wonder in the second column. Maybe they wonder if any women were explorers, or if different body cells look and work differently.

Step 6: Ask students to write their guesses in the third column.

Step 7: If you create a four-column chart using an *L* for learn, students would use the last column to write answers to their questions.

Reflect

Ask students, "How does this activity better prepare us for learning?" Listen for such comments as, "This activity starts me thinking about the subject" or "This makes me know what answers I want to be searching for," and so on.

Follow-up and Extension

1. Teach lesson 1 using art prints, colors, sounds, or smells.

2. Set up a guessing center in the classroom. Provide various kinds of guessing activities: How many? What kind? Where does it come from? Following are some ideas to get you started; you can also let students come up with guessing ideas.

   - Guess the title of an abstract work of art.

   - Enlarge a photograph of a common item until it is nearly unrecognizable and ask students to guess what it might be.

   - Guess what's in a brown paper bag by touch (perhaps a rock, a toothbrush, or marbles).

   - Guess how many paper clips in a box or in a string of clips.

   - Guess when the next fire drill will be.

   - Guess what the weather will be next week.

Applying the Strategy to Curriculum

1. Before beginning a unit of study, allow students time to look through learning materials to find answers to their questions.
2. Play three sets of music either before *or* after a unit of study. Ask students to imagine what part of the unit each musical selection represents.

Language Arts

1. Create a KWG chart after reading the first paragraph or page of a story. Ask students to write down or discuss what they already know and make predictions about what is to come.
2. Halfway through or at the end of a story, play various kinds of music and ask students to imagine the story. Let them tell you which part of the story came to mind and why.
3. Ask students to free-associate between a word you say aloud, such as *ball game, school,* or *angry,* and three sets of music you play immediately afterward. Ask them to listen to the music and imagine a story by associating the word and music. Have them write down their stories.

Physical Education

1. Before beginning a new game, make KWG charts to review the rules.
2. Make KWG charts before beginning a unit on nutrition.

Did You Know?

George Bernard Shaw once said, "What we want is to see the child in pursuit of knowledge, and not knowledge in pursuit of the child."

Strategy 3

If He, She, or It Knew Me

In Brief

These lessons help students become accustomed to hearing and learning from their inner voices by having them advise an imaginary friend and having them imagine someone advising them.

Objective

To teach students how to turn within themselves for advice by activating their inner mentors

Background

Career counselors often have clients create an imaginary mentor. The imaginary mentor might be a famous person or an imaginary person who has a compilation of admired characteristics. When people ask the imaginary mentors for advice, they actually ask themselves, but because they imagine the advice coming come from admired mentors, it often is more original than advice they might consciously give themselves.

Lesson 1: Helping an Imaginary Friend

Time

25 minutes (includes 5 minutes prep time)

Materials

a list of characters from books or of historical figures

thought journals

Preparation

Look through class materials to create a written or mental list of characters with which your class is familiar.

Focus

Ask students, "When you are in trouble or having a problem, to whom do you go for advice? Why do you go to that particular person?" Ask for volunteers to discuss their answers.

Teach

Step 1: Choose a character from the list and start a class discussion about that character. Describe the characteristics, likes and dislikes, then sum up in one sentence a problem the character is having: "Charlotte is a kind, very smart spider. She is dying and wants to help her friend Wilbur and safely lay her eggs." "Thomas Edison is a smart inventor who works very hard. He is having trouble getting this lightbulb to work."

Step 2: Ask students to pretend that they know the character personally. Assign them to write individual letters or dialogues in which they acknowledge the character's plight and offer advice as good friends.

Step 3: An alternative way to teach this lesson is to ask students to choose favorite characters from the list. Demonstrate how students should write down what one character is like and what kind of problem he or she is having. Then assign the same letter- or dialog-writing assignment.

Reflect

Ask for students to volunteer answers to the following questions: "How is your advice different from what the character actually does? If you actually knew the character, would your advice help? How might your advice change the course of events in the story or in history?"

Lesson 2: Who Can Help You?

Time

25 minutes (includes 5 minutes prep time)

Materials

the list of characters from the previous lesson

thought journals

Focus

Ask students to volunteer answers to the following questions: "When you are in trouble or having a problem, to whom do you go for advice? What kind of advice do you like best?"

Teach

Step 1: Choose one character from the list for the whole class, or ask students to pick one character each.

Step 2: Have each student write down a problem they are having or recently had. It can be a simple problem, such as she couldn't get a bike to work right, or complex, such as a pet that recently died.

Step 3: Ask students to imagine that the characters they chose are close friends who like to come to the rescue. Ask them to imagine how their friends would help them solve the problems they wrote down. Remind students that they shouldn't let their imaginary characters do or say things that the real characters would never do. For example, Charlotte would never say, "Just give up," and Edison wouldn't be able to explain how to build a jet engine. Suggest that students think about how the characters might solve the problems themselves. For example, Edison would probably persist; Charlotte might think up some clever idea.

Step 4: Assign students to write notes or letters of advice and encouragement to themselves from their friends.

Reflect

Discuss as a class answers to the following question: "How is your character's advice different from your advice to yourself? How is it the same?"

Follow-up and Extension

Have students list in their thought journals famous or everyday people they admire and want to be like. They can build their list from class materials, history units, the newspaper, or people they know.

Applying the Strategy to Curriculum

When a conflict or problem arises in class, such as students coming in late from recess or a group not working well together, discuss the problem as a class by asking for student volunteers to pretend to be literary or historical characters offering a solution.

Language Arts

1. Assign students to write dialogues between themselves and leading and minor characters in the current reading. Use this technique to increase students' understanding of a character's traits and dilemma. For example, you might say, "Write a dialog between you and Charlotte. Give her some ideas about how to solve her problem. Let her tell you what she likes or doesn't like about your idea." Or use *Sesame Street* as an example. Oscar might get angry and tell you to mind your own business. Big Bird would listen and probably like many of your ideas.

2. Assign students to write notes to a character in the reading as you complete each chapter. The notes should reflect advice, concern, admiration, or feelings about something that happened in the reading.

Social Studies

1. Have students write letters and notes to a historical character. The notes should give thoughts or advice about a specific event. For example, a letter to Benedict Arnold might suggest he side with the rebellion and tell why.

2. Assign students to write an episode in history as if they were there. Have them explain how the event would change because of their presence.

3. Have students act out a dialog between a historical figure and themselves regarding a problem or particular concern. Direct students to have the historical figure offer advice. You can keep this exercise less personal by having the class brainstorm problems typical to students of today; students can pick a problem from the list. After each student's performance, evaluate the advice as a class. Ask, "Would this character feel that way and give that advice? Why do you think so?" You can also do this exercise orally, for example, "What might Harriet Tubman say about our problem with . . . ?"

Science

1. Have students have conversations with an animal you are studying. In writing or orally, they can ask the animal questions about its behavior, appearance, and so on. Ask students to research the correct answers to their own or other students' questions. The project can be ongoing; pictures of the animal and students' questions and answers can be pinned on a bulletin board or taped to a wall.

2. Have students tell cells, asteroids, or atoms what they are supposed to do and what they should avoid. Prompt your students with questions for them to answer orally: "If we could talk to that asteroid, what would we want to know? What might it tell us? Is there a request or some advice we might like to give to the asteroid?"

3. Have students write letters to a famous scientist or inventor, or have them write a dialog between themselves and a scientist. In their writing, they discuss the feelings and actions involved with inventing something or discovering a principle.

Math

1. Have students pretend that geometric shapes have names and can talk and explain math or measurement problems. Assign students to write the dialog they imagine taking place. For example, "What exactly is a diameter?" "Well, that's my measurement from one side to the other. It's different than a radius because the radius stops at my belly button."

2. Have students pretend a famous mathematician is giving advice on how to work a problem or frustration with math. What does she tell them to do? Try this strategy as a class discussion or an individual writing assignment.

Physical Education

Have students write a dialog between a famous athlete and themselves in which the athlete explains how to improve in sports. This activity can be done individually to help the less athletic students over their stumbling blocks. You can also develop the dialog as a class to demonstrate good sportsmanship and persistence.

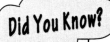

Did You Know?

In *Endangered Minds*, Jane Healy writes: "A well-nourished mind, well grounded in the precursors of wisdom as well as of knowledge, will continue to grow, learn, and develop—as long as it responds to the prickling of curiosity. Perhaps this quality, above all, is the one we should strive to preserve in all our children" (1987, 346).

Strategy 4

The Message from the Box

(adapted from Lazear 1991a)

In Brief

Students use drawing and writing to free-associate about a current topic to gain additional insight.

Time

25 minutes

Objective

To encourage intuitive comprehension of a topic by helping students interact with their intuition

Background

Intuitive and instinctual responses to subject matter can be easily stifled in the interest of filling students with information. When students are afforded time to listen to their inner voices, they often discover opinions and feelings they didn't know they had.

Materials

thought journals

crayons or other color supplies

rulers (optional)

Focus

Ask students, "How many of you sometimes hear a voice in your heads talking to you? What kinds of things do you remember that voice saying?" Some students will say the voice tells them they goofed up; others will say the voice reminds them to do things or pats them on the back when they achieve a goal.

Teach

Step 1: Pick a subject you have been studying that has many levels of understanding (the Constitution, American Indians in early America, slavery, immigration, the process of scientific discovery are all good examples).

Step 2: Ask students to draw a box about four inches by four inches in the middle of a blank page in their thought journals.

Step 3: Remind students of the subject you have been studying and summarize the major points. Ask them to take a deep breath, close their eyes, and think about that topic for a few minutes.

Step 4: Explain that as soon as any image relating to the topic comes into their minds, they should open their eyes and draw the image in the boxes on their papers. The image might be a scene or a symbol.

Step 5: Give them three to five minutes to think. Once students have drawn their images, ask them to draw three or four smaller boxes around the big box.

Step 6: Explain that in each smaller box they should draw an image that comes to mind when looking at the bigger image they drew first. No matter how silly, strange, or unrelated the other images seem, they should draw them into the other boxes.

Step 7: Give students about ten minutes to work. Ask them to look at their papers and pretend the big boxes can speak and are trying to tell them something. Ask them to concentrate and try to hear exactly what the boxes are saying.

Step 8: Explain that you want them to draw word bubbles coming from the big boxes and write the messages they heard into the bubbles.

Reflect

Ask students to share their messages with the class, and ask them, "How do you feel about the message? Does the box's message make you feel differently about the topic? How?" After all students have shared, ask them to think about where the message is really coming from.

Follow-up and Extension

Use the message from the box to gain insight into the importance of class and school rules or a field-trip learning experience, or to center the students before beginning a lesson.

Applying the Strategy to Curriculum

1. Have students use the Message from the Box activity to close a unit.
2. Use the image in the box and the message as the beginning of a unit or as a pretest activity.

Science

During a unit on inventors, use the Message from the Box to help students stop and think about the next important invention or discovery: What should it be? What could it be? What problems could be solved or fixed by the new discovery?

Language Arts

1. Have students draw an image about a main character or minor character who plays an important role.
2. Have students draw an image in the box about the setting of the story.
3. Have students draw an image in the box about the biggest problem in the story.

4. Have students listen to music and then draw any image that comes to mind in the box. When students have completed the Message from the Box activity, assign them to write a story, poem, or music about the image.

Social Studies

Give students time to think about a local current event or a news article. Have students use the Message from the Box to uncover their own opinions and feelings about the issue or event.

Strategy 5

What If . . . ?

In Brief

These lessons use the question "What If . . . ?" to encourage students to see the effect that one change can have on the course of events.

Objective

To teach students how to use cause and effect to increase their understanding of a topic

Background

Causes and effects can often occur in spiderweb or domino patterns. If students understand how one event, person, or action causes an entire string of effects, then they will have a deeper understanding of the particular topic. Answering a "what if" question about a particular topic requires basic knowledge of the subject, an understanding of the chain of events involved, and the creative ability to brainstorm new possibilities. It is an enjoyable way to test students' basic knowledge while challenging them to think creatively about causes and effects.

Lesson 1: Practicing "What If" Questions

Time

15 minutes

Materials

thought journals

Focus

Ask students, "Who can tell me a question that begins with 'What if'?" List students' questions on the chalkboard. Ask them, "How are these questions different from who, what, where, when, why, and how questions?" Allow discussion, and encourage students to understand that creativity and imagination are involved with "what if" questions.

Teach

Step 1:   Ask the class the following question, and write it on the chalkboard: "What if school started at midnight?" Allow students to brainstorm assumptions, guesses, and suggestions for a few minutes. Cluster their ideas around the question on the board. To stimulate ideas, ask them what kinds of things would have to change. Suggest that they think about how school works now—the daily schedule, the activities you do as a class and when you do them, the people who come to school—and which, if any, of these aspects would have to change.

Step 2:   Draw two columns on the chalkboard; label one "Likely" and the other "Unlikely, but Interesting." Have students copy this chart in their thought journals and follow along as you categorize answers to the question using input from the class.

Reflect

Ask students, "How is asking 'What if...?' different from asking 'What happened?'? How is it similar?" Students should understand that answering a "what happened" question requires memorizing a string of events, whereas answering "what if" means understanding the cause and effects of an event.

Lesson 2: Changing the Course of History

Time

20 to 30 minutes (includes 5 to 15 minutes prep time)

Materials

a list of main topics from a current social studies unit (for example, for a unit on the Revolutionary War: events leading to the war, key figures, famous documents)

thought journals

time line of the period

students' social studies textbooks

Preparation

Gather any reference materials (including drawings, library books, encyclopedias) that shed light on the particular topic (optional if you have textbooks and time lines, but helpful).

Write the main topics on the chalkboard.

Focus

Ask students to list specific information under each main topic on the chalkboard (for example, under "Events leading up to the war," you might list, "Boston Tea Party, Boston Massacre"). Ask students to volunteer "what if" questions relating to the topics on the board. List all the volunteered questions on the chalkboard.

Teach

Step 1:   Explain to the class that they are going to use "what if" questions to create an imaginary new history and a visual time line to go with it.

Step 2:   Choose one of the "what if" questions and erase the other questions.

Step 3:   As a class, brainstorm the aspects of the time period that would change if the "what if" question had happened (the country itself, politics, the lives of specific people, and so on). Write these aspects on the board around the question.

Step 4:   Divide the class into groups of four or five. Ask each group to work together to create a new time line for the historical period based on their answers to the question. Use any class resources you have gathered, along with textbooks and the time line you created or copied before the lesson.

Step 5:   Give students at least twenty minutes to work on their time lines, depending on the level of complexity, then ask each group to share their time line using a "this happened because this happened" format for their explanation.

Reflect

Ask students, "How does this 'what if' activity make you look at history differently?" Students should understand that single events, actions, or people can have a tremendous impact on the events that follow, whereas some have less or no impact. After a class discussion, ask students to answer in their thought journals the question "What makes an event significant?"

Follow-up and Extension

1. Assign a "what if" report in which students write one paragraph per topic area explaining how it would have changed because of the "what if."

2. Use "what if" questions to reexamine class conflicts after they have been resolved. For example, "What happened before Johnny became angry? What if Johnny had done this instead? What if Sara had chosen to act like this?"

3. Keep an ongoing list of "what if" questions on the board for students to wonder about during school.

4. To encourage students to use their imaginations, make "what if" questions part of journal assignments. The possibilities are endless: "What if everyone owned their own space shuttle?" "What if you suddenly discovered a million dollars buried in your backyard?" "What if school were canceled for a year?"

Applying Strategy

Science

1. Ask "what if" questions about scientific facts: "What if cells couldn't pass along information?" "What if leaves had no chlorophyll?" "What if all fossils crumbled and disappeared after one hundred years?" "What if your brain were missing the hypothalamus?" Allow students the time and resources to investigate the answers.

2. Ask what if particular inventions or discoveries had never been made.

Language Arts

1. Periodically during each reading selection, ask a "what if" question to encourage students to think creatively about how a story could change.

2. Use "what if" questions as prewriting exercises to allow students to rewrite familiar stories: "What if Cinderella were a man?" "What if Little Red Riding Hood had ears and sharp teeth?"

3. Ask students, "What if all words were spelled the way they sound?" Assign students to write phonetic spellings for their vocabulary and spelling words, then have them check and correct their phonetic spellings against those in a dictionary.

4. Watch *It's a Wonderful Life* or *A Christmas Carol* and discuss as a class the "what if" question behind the movie.

Social Studies

1. Repeat the focus exercise and step 2 from lesson 2 for each new social studies unit. Assign students to fill in the blanks in the following statements: "The most important change would be _____ because _____.

   The most interesting change could be _____ because _____."

2. Ask "what if" questions to cement students' understanding of the importance of events or people to the course of history.

3. As a class, examine how a specific event would play out with the absence of one key player.

Math

1. Ask "what if" questions about steps in a computation to increase students' understanding of why they must do computations in a particular way: "What if you don't flip over the second fraction when dividing?" "What if you don't carry the remainder?"

2. As a class, create a "what if" bar graph about the changes in the cost of foods in the event of various crises: "What if most U.S. fruit crops were destroyed by a virus?" "What if we have a tree shortage?" This strategy can start as a quick lesson in hypothesizing: the price of paper would go up or down comparatively. You can extend the lesson by having students research what the answers might be (for example, by finding out the difference in price between fruit grown in the United States and that grown in other countries, or between recycled paper and first-run paper). Ask students to brainstorm where they might find the information: grocery store? business pages in the newspaper? an economics department at the local college?

7

Verbal-Linguistic Intelligence

Verbal-linguistic intelligence focuses on the use of words in reading writing, speaking, and listening. Poets, writers, public speakers, and editors use this intelligence to communicate meaningfully and powerfully.

Development of the verbal-linguistic intelligence is already a standard component of traditional school curricula, so this book offers few verbal-linguistic strategies, all of which encourage enjoyable and expressive use of words. Beyond the lessons in this book, I recommend that you combine other intelligence areas with verbal-linguistic learning whenever it makes sense in your curriculum: sing songs, write captions for original cartoons, act out a play, and so on.

Did You Know?

The word *butterfly* used to be *flutterby*. Ask your students: "Why do you think it changed? Which is a better name?"

Strategy 1

How Words Grow

In Brief

In lesson 1 students listen to the poem "Jabberwocky" by Lewis Carroll and then try to find definitions for some of the nonsense words he uses. In lesson 2 students combine and recombine common word roots, prefixes, and suffixes to create new words.

Objective

To encourage students to pay attention to the sounds and structures of words, which will help them remember vocabulary

Background

Poets love to play with words. Prose writers write and revise until their sentences have just the right ring. The people who choose these professions manage to retain some of their childlike enjoyment of the sounds words make. This strategy takes advantage of children's natural inclination to hear rhythms in language—words in rhyme, words with a beat, and nonsense words—to teach about word structure.

Use really long words made up of easily discernible prefixes, roots, and suffixes as word puzzles for students to solve. Write one on the board every day or week, and give a prize to everyone who can figure out what the word means without using a dictionary. Some ideas are *antidisestablishmentarianism* (opposition to the withdrawal of government support), *pneumoultramicroscopicsilicovolcanoconiosis* (coal miners' lung disease contracted from breathing underground fumes), *gephydrophobia* (fear of crossing bridges).

Lesson 1: Creating Words

Time

30 minutes (includes 5 minutes prep time)

Materials

thought journals or blank paper

one copy for each student of Lewis Carroll's "Jabberwocky"

Preparation

Make copies of "Jabberwocky."

Focus

Ask students to close their eyes while you read "Jabberwocky" through once. Ham it up! Read with expression and inflection, especially of the nonsensical words. Ask for volunteers to read the poem a second time, using one volunteer per stanza.

Teach

Step 1: Ask students to pick out real words in the poem. Are there any nonsense words that sound or look real? Make a list of these real-sounding nonsense words on the chalkboard.

Step 2: Ask students to read the poem to themselves, choose five to ten nonsense words, and make up a meaning for each. Ask them to think of "real" synonyms for the nonsense words.

Step 3: Read stanzas of the poem using the replacement words the students came up with. Ask students, "Does the new poem work as well? Is it as fun to hear and read? Why or why not?"

Reflect

Ask students to write an entry in their thought journals about why they think Lewis Carroll wrote this poem. Ask students, "Can you think of any other authors who write nonsense poems?"

Lesson 2: Creating Words

Time

30 minutes (includes 5 minutes prep time)

Materials

thought journals or papers

one copy for each student of the list of common word prefixes, roots, and suffixes (page 182)

Preparation

Make copies of the list. Copy the list onto the chalkboard.

Focus

Ask students, "If we encounter an unfamiliar word, how can we figure out its meaning?" Try to elicit these answers: its context, a dictionary, the meanings of its various parts (suffix, root, prefix).

Teach

Step 1: Give students the list of roots, prefixes, and suffixes.

Step 2: Ask students to think of words that use these parts.

Jabberwocky

'Twas brillig and the slithy toves
   Did gyre and gimble in the wabe:
All mimsy were the borogoves,
   And the mome raths outgrabe.

"Beware the Jabberwock, my son!
   The jaws that bite, the claws that catch!
Beware the Jubjub bird, and shun
   The frumious Bandersnatch!"

He took his vorpal sword in hand;
   Long time the manxome foe he sought—
So rested he by the Tumtum tree,
   And stood awhile in thought.

And, as in uffish thought he stood,
   The Jabberwock, with eyes aflame,
Came whiffling through the tulgey wood,
   And Burbled as it came!

One, two! One, two! And through and through
   The vorpal blade went snicker-snack!
He left it dead, and with its head
   He went galumphing back.

"And hast thou slain the Jabberwock?
   Come to my arms, my beamish boy!
O frabjous day! Callooh! Callay!"
   He chortled in his joy.

'Twas brillig and the slithy toves
   Did gyre and gimble in the wabe:
All mimsy were the borogoves,
   And the mome raths outgrabe.

Step 3: Ask students what the made-up word *aftereater* could mean. Dessert? Someone who eats at night? What about *unseement*? A hidden object? Or a decision not to look?

Step 4: Assign students to make up words by mixing and matching prefixes, roots, and suffixes. Ask them to list in their thought journals each new word and its meaning, which should make sense according to the meanings of the word parts they use.

Step 5: Have students share some of their new word ideas with the class.

Reflect

Questions to ask the class after this exercise include the following: "What sounds do you like in a word?" "Do you like the sound of words with lots of syllables or not?"

Follow-up and Extension

Brainstorm nonsense words for class use that will mean "clean-up time" or "stop and listen." Have the class vote on which word to use for each meaning.

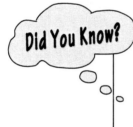

Did You Know?

A *callithump* is a large parade . . . what a wonderful word! Find more fun-sounding words to share with your students.

Applying the Strategy to Curriculum

Science

1. Discover as a class how new stars get their names.

2. Ask the class to think about the following questions: "What happens when new inventions are made or new chemicals are formed? How do they get their names? Does every language give new inventions or chemicals different names?" As a class, find out the answers.

Language Arts

1. As new prefixes, roots, and suffixes are introduced in readings or spelling lessons, practice their meanings by using them to make more nonsense words.

2. Have the class think up nonsense words to express frustration, happiness, pride, and other emotions.

3. Assign students to make up a nonsense rhyme like "Jabberwocky."

4. Engage the class in writing a list of things for which there are no words, such as the dust that gathers on top of light bulbs, the little flattened part of shoe heels, fingerprints on photographs, or gum on the bottom of shoes. Make up words for these things, and write a class poem or story using the new words.

Math

1. As a class, brainstorm ways to use math symbols as prefixes, suffixes, or roots for a math "language." For instance, *X* could mean "multiplied," so *X-rock-ology* would mean the study of newly formed rocks. Or + as a root could mean "add the prefix and suffix," so "pre+ment" would mean "an action before," and so on.

2. Use the following fill-in-the-blank questions to make up new words using math operational signs:

(prefix) + (root) + (suffix) = (a new word)

(existing word) - (prefix or suffix) = (a new word)

- (existing word) = (its opposite)

Social Studies

1. Create new words for historical events that never happened, for example the new country that would have been created had the South won the Civil War.

2. This exercise is especially useful during a unit on geographical terminology (*peninsula*, *bay*, and so on). Have students independently draw or write about an imaginary country. Make up names for the geographic areas, such as *Peanut Peninsula* and *Mambo Mountains.* Draw a map of the imaginary place and label its geographic features.

Did You Know?

Clue originally meant "ball of thread," which would explain the existence of the phrase "unraveling a mystery." What are some other word histories that tell stories?

Strategy 2

Very Punny

In Brief

Students learn that the success of a pun is based on unusual and funny word associations. Students brainstorm word associations in order to create their own puns.

Time

15 minutes

> **REMINDER**
>
> Some classes and students catch on to the skill of making puns, whereas other classes need lots of examples and lots of practice. Gauge your class's comfort at each step of this lesson and consider repeating it before moving on if you sense that they are hesitant.

Objective

To increase vocabulary by brainstorming associated words and creating puns

Background

Children start to understand puns as early as preschool. Because puns depend on word associations and rhyme, it is an enjoyable way to play with words and teach language skills. Puns can also be used as mnemonic devices to help students remember facts or vocabulary for tests.

Materials

thought journals

joke and riddle books (optional)

Focus

Tell students a few puns: "What is a pig's favorite pet?" (a ham-ster) "What kind of witch likes the beach?" (a sand-wich)

How Words Grow:
Prefixes, Roots, and Suffixes

Prefixes

un (opposite: **un**do, **un**safe)
re (again: **re**do, **re**read)
fore (in front: **fore**word, **fore**cast)
mega (a million, or very big: **mega**byte, **mega**phone)
after (happens later: **after**shock, **after**taste)
bio (life: **bio**logy, **bio**graphy)
tele (far: **tele**phone, **tele**scope)

Roots

see
meet
do
scope (to look)
eat
graph (to write)
know

Suffixes

ment (an action or a condition: develop**ment**, involve**ment**)
ed (already happened: walk**ed**, slic**ed**)
ing (happening now: walk**ing**, slic**ing**)
er (someone or something who does an action: walk**er**, slic**er**)
y (having a quality: cloud**y**, cheer**y**)
logy (the study of something: bio**logy**, meteoro**logy**)
ful (filled with, full of something: thank**ful**, spite**ful**)

Teach

Step 1: Explain that a pun is a kind of joke that is based on a play on words. It will be easy for them to make up puns once they understand the patterns and develop a list of associated words.

Step 2: Tell students that they are going to spend time working as a class to make up their own puns. Begin by making up puns about rabbits.

Step 3: Explain that the first word to play with is *rabbit* itself. As a class, brainstorm synonyms for *rabbit,* words that sound like *rabbit,* words that have *rabbit* in them, and so on. Some ideas: *rabbit, habit, bunny, buns, bunt, Easter Bunny, funny, runny, rabid, ribbit* (sound a frog makes), *grab it, robot, hare, hair,* and so on.

Step 4: Brainstorm words about rabbits: *carrot, carat, carry it, scare it, bunny hop, jump, hop, sock hop, cottontail, Peter, snail, rotten snail,* and so on.

Step 5: Prompt the class to find ideas for puns in the list. Some ideas follow: "What do you call an automated bunny?" (a rabbot) "What's a rabbit's favorite party?" (a sock hop) "What did Ms. Rabbit say when Mr. Rabbit proposed?" ("How many carrots in the diamond?") "What is a rabbit Halloween party called?" (A s-carrot party). Continue until you've exhausted all possibilities.

Reflect

After you've completed a couple lessons on puns with your students, ask them, "What kind of words make the best puns? What's the trick to making up a good pun?" Some students will understand that a successful pun uses words with double meanings, words that sound alike, or words that catch you off guard.

Follow-up and Extension

Have a best puns award or display, and let students work on new puns to add to the exhibit when they have completed their work.

Applying the Strategy to Curriculum

Math

Create math puns for your students to solve. For example, "What did the equal sign say to the plus and minus signs?" ("You guys decide which way to go—I'll just get us there.") "What deal did the greater and lesser signs make?" ("I'll eat my number, you tickle yours.") "How many plus signs does it take to turn 8 and 8 into 64?" ("One, just tip it to its side.")

Science

Use puns and word associations to help students remember vocabulary and concepts. For example, have students fill in the blanks of the following question using objects or concepts they are currently studying, then come up with an answer to the joke. "What did the _____ say to the _____?" (magnet to the wood, H_2 to the O, pulley to the weight, and so on).

Language Arts

Write puns about characters or stories you are reading.

REMINDER Whether we like it or not, our students watch television and play video games. They will most likely draw on characters and events from these activities when creating puns. As long as they're learning the lesson, encourage rather than discourage them since they will draw more easily on what they know best.

Social Studies

1. Use puns to help students remember vocabulary, important dates, or geographical places. Puns can lend a humorous angle to social studies material. Work as a class to brainstorm a list of words and phrases associated with the name of a famous historical person or event. Then use the list to create puns. For example, a list of associated words for the Boston Tea Party includes *Boston, Boston baked beans, Boston cream pie, tea party, tea, cream and sugar, Indians, revolution, steep the tea, one lump or two, boiling kettle, teapot, Republican party, Democratic party.* Possible puns include, "Which party had the first and greatest influence over the U.S. government?" (the Boston Tea Party) "What did King George say when he heard about the tea in Boston Harbor?" ("The colonists' kettle must be boiling over!")

2. During a unit on exploration, write puns for each explorer. Start with this question: "What did Balboa first say when _____

   _____

   _____ ?"

3. Write puns for famous events and historical periods such as the Mayflower's landing, Columbus's voyage, the gold rush, the Salem witch trials, the Puritans and Quakers, or the pioneers. "What did the _____ say to the _____?" (Puritan to the Algonquin, gold miner to the pioneer, and so on).

Strategy 3

Freewrite for Thinking

In Brief

This strategy introduces students to the concept of freewriting, which—when used regularly—can increase students' ease with the writing process and their confidence in their own ideas.

Time

10 minutes for each freewriting session

Objective

To use train-of-thought writing skills to get ideas out of students' heads and onto paper

Background

The left brain often associates itself with writing because it is sequential and analytical. If your goal is to write creatively or to produce new ideas, however, the right brain needs to be more actively involved. A freewriting activity bores the left brain because it seems to have no direction, no clear role. Freewriting is a technique many writers use to get started on an idea or to overcome writer's block. It is particularly effective first thing in the morning before the left brain is wide awake. The right brain then has a better chance of leading the process and developing some interesting concepts.

REMINDER

Students need to practice freewriting regularly in order to improve and reap the benefits. Always give students a solid ten minutes for a freewriting session; it takes that long for the best brain juices to start flowing. Students will have a hard time freewriting on a topic they know nothing about. Before assigning a topic, think about whether lack of information will be a stumbling block, especially if you're going to use freewriting as a part of a social studies or science lesson plan.

Follow Your Thoughts

Materials

thought journals

Focus

Ask students, "How do you think writers and artists get their ideas?" Allow some time for class discussion. Then explain that one method writers use is called *freewriting*. Explain that it's like a brainstorm that you do alone; you try to write down everything your brain says about a particular topic without trying to filter any of it out because it might be "dumb" or repetitive, or because someone else already thought of it.

Teach

Step 1:   Pick one of the following topics or think up your own topic and write it on the chalkboard: "My life as a chicken," "The food that crawled off my plate," "My favorite sport," "My favorite place," "If I were queen of the world," "Peanuts."

Step 2:   Tell students they have ten minutes just to write and write on this topic. Because it is a brainstorm and not a finished writing sample they do not need to worry about spelling, grammar, paragraphs, or other mechanics. In fact, if while they are writing they get distracted by a better idea they can just write away on the better idea without finishing the sentence they were working on. If they run out of thoughts they should not stop. Tell them to listen to the voices in their heads and write whatever the voices say to them, or write the word *write* over and over until something new pops into their head. Ask them to leave their erasers out of this activity. I call the eraser "the left brain talking."

Step 3:   After ten minutes, call time. Ask a few students to share one or two sentences from their freewriting session that they like (for example, interesting words, an interesting concept, something they wrote that surprised them).

Step 4:   After a session, students can highlight parts they like with yellow crayon, pick out parts to use in a story or poem, or put the journal away until the next session.

Reflect

Involve the class in a discussion about the following questions: "How is freewriting freer than regular classroom writing assignments?" "Is freewriting more like a sports car or a bicycle? Why?"

Follow-up and Extension

1. Schedule a ten-minute freewriting session on a topic at the start of every language arts period.

2. When assigning any kind of written report, have students freewrite on their chosen or assigned topic before starting to write the actual report.

3. Use freewriting to come up with ideas for a class play or poem about a specific subject. Make sure that students know something about the topic before freewriting, though. After freewriting, students can use yellow crayon to highlight interesting parts that they might want to use in the play or poem.

Strategy 4

Persuasive Speeches

In Brief

Students discuss their ideas about what makes a person change his or her mind, then practice their reasoning skills by trying to find logical support for crazy ideas.

Objectives

To give students practice in the art and science of persuasion

To encourage students to be creative in their approaches to an argument

Background

Skilled use of persuasive language is the height of verbal-linguistic intelligence. To be able to convince someone to change positions requires a strong argument and an arguer with well-developed verbal and linguistic abilities. This strategy seeks to give students regular practice debating and arguing.

Lesson 1: Changing Your Mind

Time

15 to 30 minutes

Materials

thought journals (for taking notes)

Focus

Ask students, "Has anyone ever convinced you to change your mind? When? How?" Allow students to volunteer answers.

Teach

Step 1: Tell students that the lesson focuses on persuasion, which is the act of convincing someone to change his or her mind.

Step 2: Ask students, "What are some of the ways we can try to change another person's mind?" Write a list of students' ideas on the chalkboard. Encourage such answers as common sense, logic, fear, bribery, appealing to someone's better nature, and appealing to someone's self-interest.

Step 3: Ask students, "When someone is trying to change your mind about something, what kinds of arguments convince you?" Write students' responses on the board next to their responses to the first question.

Step 4: Divide the class into groups of four. Explain that each group is going to pretend that they have just discovered a treasure map. But according to the map, they must cross through someone's private property to get to the treasure. Ask the students to work together for five to ten minutes to come up with three arguments that will convince the property owner to let them through.

Step 5: When time is up, ask students to share their arguments, then say: "Now, I want you to imagine that the property owner is a gardener who spends hours caring for his plants and flowers. Does that change your arguments?" Give students a few more minutes in their groups to discuss the question, then ask them to share their ideas.

Step 6: Repeat the exercise again, telling students that you've just found out that the property owner is actually an archaeologist doing a really important dig. Will their arguments change?

Step 7: Once students understand the concept of how a successful argument changes to suit the listener, ask them to come up with arguments for the following situations:

- You want to convince students they can no longer run on the playground grass because it is dying.

- You want to convince your brother or sister to lend you a stereo.

- You want to convince your teacher to extend recess five minutes.

Reflect

Ask students, "How does thinking about the other person's needs and ideas change the way you phrase your argument?"

Lesson 2: Crazy Arguments

Time

15 minutes

Focus

Ask students, "Have you ever heard anyone give an argument that you couldn't believe you were hearing because it was so crazy?" Let students share their stories, and ask if they thought the arguer was successful or unsuccessful, and why.

Teach

Step 1: Tell students you're going to ask them to try to find logical arguments to support crazy ideas. Explain that the goal is to stick to reasonable, persuasive arguments, even though the issue at hand is illogical.

Step 2: The first crazy topic is "Why we should wear our clothes inside out on Fridays." Give students a minute to search for a logical argument, then let volunteers share their ideas. Ask students to raise their hands when they have ideas to share (this strategy is also good to use with classroom debates). Encourage freewheeling thinking, give special praise to particularly original or strangely logical ideas, and let the debate continue as long as students are thinking up reasonable arguments.

Step 3: Try other crazy arguments, either in this lesson or as a follow-up. Some ideas to get you started follow:

Why we should get rid of our school desks

Why everyone should pack peanuts in their lunch

Why roller skates should be the only vehicle allowed on roads

Why every school should have its own roller coaster

Reflect

Start a classroom discussion by asking the following question: "When is a persuasive argument all hot air and no balloon?"

Follow-up and Extension

Organize regular classroom debates on such topics as, "The best physical education game for our class" or "Why every day should be a weekend day."

Applying the Strategy to Curriculum

Science

1. Have students square off (pick two students, or divide the class into two sides) and debate whether particular modern technologies are good or bad for the world.

2. Organize a classroom debate on the topic of which invention, the car or the rocket ship, changed the world more.

Language Arts

1. Have students debate which of two reading assignments is better. Allow two students to debate for the class, or divide the class into two teams. Encourage them to come up with specific qualities that make a book good and organize the debate around those qualities.

2. Organize a classroom debate on the issue of which is more important, good spelling or good grammar.

3. Ask students to argue persuasively on behalf of the antagonist in the current reading selection.

4. Have students create a persuasive argument for why a protagonist should not be successful in a mission.

Math

Draw students' attention to some of the similarities between verbal logic and mathematical equations (the phrase "If this and this are true, then this is true" can be represented by writing $x + y = z$). Ask students if they think they can represent very simple verbal arguments with mathematical symbols and how they would do so. Show them the following examples, and work as a class to come up with others.

fruit + Cheerios + milk = a balanced breakfast

student - homework = recess study club

school day - (recess + lunch) = learning time

horse + cart = (transportation + hauling) x many

Encourage students to come up with their own ideas.

Social Studies

1. Have students pretend to be historical figures trying to win a persuasive historical argument. Be sure the debate concerns a current unit. Possibilities include Columbus arguing for financial support for his trip while Queen Isabella argues against it; a loyalist and a patriot argue whether Benedict Arnold is truly a traitor; King George and Benjamin Franklin argue the merits of taxation without representation; an Algonquian and a Puritan debate the use of fences around property. Encourage students to ham it up when they reenact the debate, or turn the lesson into a play.

2. As a class project, try to find reasons to support crazy arguments about historical events. For example, why the colonists should have gone along with King George's taxes, why Levi Strauss should have joined the gold rush instead of making pants, and so on.

3. Have students create persuasive arguments for changing the course of history.

4. To encourage comparative historical analysis, arrange class debates that set events from different historical periods in opposition: Which was more important to U.S. history, the Revolutionary War or the Civil War? Who was a better president, George Washington or Abraham Lincoln?

8

Mathematical-Logical Intelligence

The mathematical-logical intelligence focuses on working with numbers, sequences of events, and organizing information. Mathematicians, scientists, statisticians, accountants, and economists use mathematical-logical intelligence to make predictions, design programs and systems, measure quantities, and test hypotheses.

Like verbal-linguistic intelligence, mathematical-logical intelligence already plays a major role in traditional education. You can use the few strategies in this chapter to strengthen students' mathematical-logical skills by igniting the organization-processing centers of the brain through exercises in patterning, predicting, and charting. In addition to using these lessons, I recommend that you look for math lessons that incorporate other intelligences so students can actively utilize additional parts of their brains at the same time. Examples of multiple intelligence math lessons are *tangrams* (spatial intelligence), *word problems* (verbal intelligence), *dividing rhythms and beats* (musical intelligence), and *manipulatives* (physical).

Strategy 1

Puzzles and Patterns

In Brief

Students are first introduced to the idea that patterns are all around them, then they use patterns to solve increasingly complex problems, and finally they create their own patterns and puzzles.

Objective

To teach students to use patterns as a learning strategy for a variety of curriculum areas

Background

The human brain is naturally motivated to see and use patterns. This strategy harnesses that motivation for classroom learning.

Lesson 1: Patterns Are Everywhere

Time

30 minutes

Materials

thought journals or writing paper

regularly planned lesson in any subject area

REMINDER

Some students will love this kind of thinking, but it will frustrate others. Do not require puzzle-making; students who like it will bring in lots of ideas, which will encourage less-interested students to try it out.

Focus

Write the following number series on the chalkboard. Reveal the series to students for two minutes, and ask them to try to memorize as many as possible:

1, 5, 9, 13, 17, 21
1, 4, 2, 1, 2, 8, 3, 5, 4, 2, 4, 9

Cover the numbers, and ask for volunteers to show off their memorization skills. Let a few students try, then explain that each series has a pattern that can help them memorize it. Show them the combinations again and help them find the patterns. The first pattern adds four to each number; the second pattern begins with fourteen, then adds seven, with digits separated by commas. Have students try to find the patterns and complete the following series:

blue, black, yellow, green, blue, black, yellow, green, blue,

_____, _____, _____

Answer: black, yellow, green.

Pattern: repetition of blue, black, yellow, green

1 2 1 2 1 1 2 1 2 2 1 2 1 2 3 1 2 1 2 4 1 2 1 2 5 1

_____ _____ _____

Answer: 2 1 2 6

Pattern: 1 2 1 2 followed by 1, then 2, and so on

10, 29, 38, 47, 56, 65, 74,

_____, _____, _____

Answer: 83, 92, 101

Pattern: tens digit increases by one, ones digit decreases by one

3, 9, 14, 18, 21,

_____, _____

Answer: 23, 24

Pattern: +6, +5, +4, +3

Ask students which pattern was easiest/hardest to find.

Teach

Step 1: Explain that patterns are everywhere. Ask students to write in their thought journals a list of places where they might find patterns. Possibilities include art, wallpaper, advertising, musical rhythms, melodies, the chorus of a song, clothing designs, chapter headings in a book, alphabetical or numerical listings (the phone book or a dictionary), history, people doing "the wave" at a stadium, cells in a body, behavior.

Step 2: Explain to students that by working at finding patterns they are using both sides of their brains and increasing their brains' capacity. Offer to put up one new pattern on the chalkboard every day for them to guess during the course of the day.

Reflect

Ask students in what ways they can use patterns to help them learn.

Lesson 2: Word Puzzles

Time

35 minutes (includes 5 minutes prep time)

Materials

thought journals or writing paper

one copy for each student of each of the following puzzles

Preparation

Make copies of the word puzzles. Write the puzzles on the chalkboard.

Focus

Give students copies of the first set of word puzzles and ask them to decipher them. Answers are *eggs over easy; time after time or time and time again; head over heels; I understand; he's beside himself; job opening; scrambled eggs; a break in the schedule; man overboard.*

Teach

Step 1: Ask students to find any patterns to these word puzzles. Ask them to write out the answers to the puzzles using words and to look for patterns in the kinds of words being used. You want them to see that the puzzles all use directional or action words, for example, *beside, under, over, split, scrambled, opening.*

Step 2: Ask students to brainstorm more directional or action words that might be used in word puzzles. Possibilities include *below, on top, high, low, above, stretched, separated, broken, fat, tall.*

Puzzles 1

eggs	TIME TIME	**head**
———		———
easy		**heels**
stand	**he'shimself**	J OB
———		
I		
GEGS	**SCHE/DULE**	man
		———
		board

Puzzles 2

HEA RT   **mind**
               ———————
               matter

R / E / A / D

Step 3: Give students the second set of puzzles to solve and see if they can do it more easily. Answers are *broken heart; read between the lines; mind over matter.*

Step 4: Have students make up their own word puzzles using directional or action words.

Reflect

Ask students, "What do you think happens inside your brain when you see a word puzzle? Does your brain react differently from the way it reacts when you are asked a question?"

Lesson 3: Making Patterns with Colors and Sounds

Time

30 minutes

Materials

graph paper

crayons or colored pencils

rhythm instruments (optional)

Focus

Ask for a volunteer to give a definition of *rhythm*. Solicit responses until students understand that a rhythm is a regularly repeating series of sounds. Ask for a student volunteer to tap a rhythm on a desk. Have the whole class repeat it. Ask students, "How is a rhythm like a pattern of colors?" Encourage students to understand that colors can be like notes or tones, and that a rhythm can be a long or short sequence before it repeats.

Teach

Step 1: Pass out graph paper and crayons. Have students create a simple two- or three-color pattern on four to five lines of the paper (for example, red, yellow, red, yellow, red; or green, green, blue, yellow, green, green, blue, yellow).

Step 2: Ask students if they can turn their color patterns into rhythm patterns. How would they do it? Some students will suggest speeds for colors, or perhaps sounds (snap, clap, or slap). Some will suggest having different people play different colors. Allow them to experiment and perform.

Step 3: Write three or four number series on the board and ask students to re-create them using rhythms or colored patterns.

Some patterns to include:

2, 4, 6, 8 (clap every other beat)

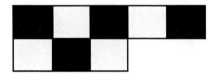

10, 1, 9, 2, 8, 3, 7, 4 (on paper color 10 red, 1 blue, 9 red, 2 blue, and so on)

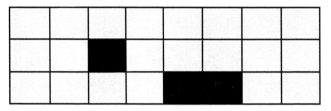

+5, -1, +4, -2, +3, -1 (stomp pluses, clap minuses)

Step 4: Allow time for experimentation, performance, and discussion.

Follow-up and Extension

Challenge students to notice patterns in the way people talk or act. Before a field trip, tell students that a prize will be awarded to the student who finds the most patterns during the trip.

Applying the Strategy to Curriculum

1. Create word puzzles that complement a unit being studied, and encourage students to create some, too. Examples include "Wilbur the pig is afraid of becoming ebgagcson" (scrambled eggs and bacon);

             A S M A G
            A   G
           I   E
           L world L   (Magellan sailed around the world.)
           E   L
             D N A

2. Before starting any regularly scheduled lesson, tell students to watch for and write down any patterns they notice as you go through the lesson. They might notice that each paragraph indents, that there is a pattern of one book on each student's desk, or that the teacher has a pattern of stopping and looking up after every paragraph. Encourage students to look for patterns within the material itself; they may notice a pattern of moving to the new world for religious freedom or that a character behaves in a certain pattern. At the end of a lesson ask students to share their notes with

the class; write students' ideas on the chalkboard and compliment students who found unusual, subtle patterns that other students did not catch.

Science

1. Science lessons are a great place to look for patterns to use for learning, since nature is full of repetition and regularity. Have students look for patterns when they study cells, layers of Earth, or seasons.

2. Ask students if they discern any patterns in the scientific process. Encourage them to see that the pattern is in the repetition of test and hypothesis. As a class, discuss the pattern and why it exists.

Language Arts

1. Ask students to look for patterns in characters' behavior. Do they always stand up for the underdog? Do they repeatedly pace, blush, stutter, or complain? Do any character patterns change in the course of a story?

2. Ask students to find patterns in the settings of a reading. Is it always dark when something scary is about to happen?

3. Have students look for patterns in poetry; draw their attention to the number of syllables, the placement of rhyming words, the length of the stanzas. Then talk about where in a poem the patterns get broken. Ask students, "Is there a reason to break the pattern in that spot?"

Math

1. Have students create color or musical patterns and then translate them into math formulas.

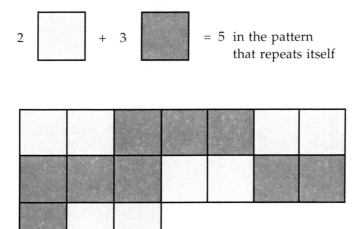

2. Create visual geometric patterns to teach vocabulary and mathematical concepts such as various shapes, sizes, and planes. I use this especially with compasses. Following is a sample lesson.

> *Fold your page in half and in half again. Open it and find the center point of the page (where the two creases meet). Set your compass to a one-inch radius and draw a circle using the center point of the page as your circle's center point. Use the four points where the perimeter of your circle intersects with the folds in the page as new center points for new circles. Draw four more circles with one-inch radii. How much does the diameter of one of the circles measure? How do you know?*

Let them color the designs when they are finished. Students can create various designs in the same way using rulers or compasses. Beginning students need to watch you do the steps as well as listen to the instructions. More advanced or practiced students will be able to follow your oral instructions.

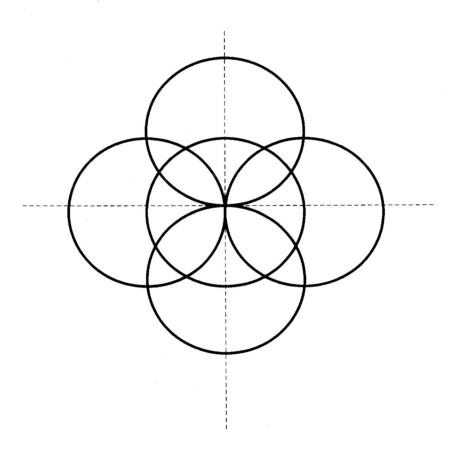

Social Studies

1. Ask students to find patterns in a history textbook. For example, time lines at the beginnings of chapters, a test at the back, review questions before the test.

2. Ask students what they think the following saying means: "History repeats itself." Ask if they can think of examples to prove or disprove that statement. Possibly assign a report on the topic.

3. Ask students to look for patterns of immigration to the United States. For each major time period of immigration, have them make a series of bar graphs and pie charts to answer the following questions: "How many of each ethnic group came during the period?" "What kinds of transportation were used?" "What were the primary reasons for immigrating?" "How did they live and work once they arrived?"

Strategy 2

Predicting and Testing

In Brief

In lesson 1 students learn the steps involved in making accurate predictions. In lesson 2 they learn how to test their predictions for accuracy.

Did You Know?

Studies have shown that we can use frogs to predict the weather with 80 percent accuracy. In China tests revealed that if frogs croak on a nice day it will rain in two days, if frogs croak after rain the weather will be nice, and if frogs don't croak when it is overcast, it will keep raining (Louis 1983, 181).

Objective

To develop students' abilities to make logical predictions and test accuracy

Background

Predicting and checking for accuracy builds the ability to plan ahead. These two skills are the cornerstones of experimentation—a prediction followed by a test to determine accuracy—and forecasting—a prediction followed by a period of waiting to determine accuracy.

Lesson 1: Seeing into the Future

Time

15 minutes

Materials

thoughts journals or writing paper

Focus

Ask students, "If you predicted that there was going to be a storm and then a storm came, would that mean you have the power to see into the future?" Discuss their answers, asking some of the following questions: "Why might you predict that a storm was coming in the first place?" "If someone asked you if you thought a storm was coming, what would you base your answer on?"

Teach

Divide students into groups of about four and ask them to brainstorm various guesses and predictions that can be made and tested. They should write down a list of the kinds of predictions and how they would test the guess. A list might include the following: How many marbles? Count them. The weather tomorrow? Wait until tomorrow. What is the answer to a math problem? Work out the problem. What is the most popular kind of ice cream at school? Survey the school.

Reflect

Ask students, "How does making predictions change the way you begin to look at or study a topic?" Students often recognize that it increases excitement because they want to see if they are right. They may also recognize that if you plan to test predictions, you need to set up the studies carefully.

Lesson 2: Predicting and Testing

Time

15 minutes

Materials

thought journals or writing paper

Focus

Ask the class what kinds of predictions can be solved by doing an opinion survey. Answers might include what people like to eat, what people watch on television, and how people feel about a particular event.

Teach

Step 1: Ask students to think about how they would find the answer to the following question: "What is the sport that people most like to watch?"

Step 2: Ask if they think it is possible to ask every person in the world his or her opinion. Explain that since it is not feasible to interview or gather the opinions of all people, they must narrow the scope of the survey so that the question actually has a chance of being answered.

Step 3: Brainstorm ways to narrow the focus of the question: "Which sport do students at our school prefer to watch: baseball, soccer, or gymnastics?"

Step 4: Ask students to brainstorm ways to find the answer to the question. Most students will suggest taking a survey or asking around.

Step 5: Divide the class into groups of about four. Ask each group to design a way to survey the school. Have each group present their plan to the rest of the class.

Step 6: As a class, discuss each group's plan to determine if the plan would work. Look for logistical problems, such as the following: If a group suggests taking the survey during recess, how can they avoid asking the same person twice? If they suggest counting hands in classrooms, ask if they think some students might just pick what everyone else picks instead of voting for their true favorite. What could go wrong with the idea of visiting homes to see what sport students watch? As you discuss each group's plan, ask the class if it would generate accurate information. Let students discuss and pick the most feasible method.

Step 7: If feasible at your school, allow students to perform the survey and look at the results.

Reflect

Have the class discuss the following questions: "Is a survey a good way to check predictions?" "If you want to design a really accurate survey, what kinds of qualities should it have?"

Follow-up and Extension

1. Ask students to predict what lessons you will teach the next day or what you will include on tests, which gives them practice figuring out what is most important to learn and understand.

2. Have students predict which television show is a school favorite and then conduct a survey using the most accurate method as determined in lesson 2.

Applying the Strategy to Curriculum

1. Have the class design an opinion survey about something related to their studies. Possible questions include the following: "How many people have seen the movie that goes with the book we are reading?" "Which American Indian tribe do you think is the most interesting to learn about?" Have students work in small groups to come up with a way to conduct a survey, then discuss as a class the feasibility of each group's idea. Predict the results, then have each group conduct the survey using their method. Graph each group's results on a bar graph and compare and contrast any differences.

2. Assign students to work in groups of four to five to think about predictions they could make about a topic. Each group should make a list of possible predictions and ways to test each one. The lists will be much shorter than the lists students made in lesson 1, and there will be more discussion about the best way to test the guesses. The first time students undertake this exercise, you may want to pick the topic to get them started. On page 212 are examples of topics, possible predictions, and ways to test each prediction.

Science

1. Hypothesize about an experiment before conducting the experiment. After conducting the experiment, discuss what went right or wrong with the hypothesis or the experiment itself and how that affected the results. Is your hypothesis correct? Incorrect? Hard to tell from the results?

Subject: Revolutionary War

Predictions	**Tests**
King George's lifestyle or favorite food?	Do research using biographies.
What if there had been no war?	Study similar pairs of countries where no revolution happened.
How do the English feel now?	Write letters to English newspapers.

Subject: Fractions

Predictions	**Tests**
How often are fractions used at work?	Do a survey of working adults.
The answer to a math problem?	Do the problem or use a calculator.

2. Predict the next major computer technology to hit the market. Post a list of students' predictions in the classroom and ask students to bring in newspaper articles about any new technologies.

Language Arts
1. At the beginning of a story, have students predict how the story will end or how a character will change.
2. Ask students to look at the cover of a book and make predictions about the contents.
3. Look through illustrations and make predictions about what is happening at that point in the story.
4. Conduct a classroom survey to find out students' favorite books or movies. Make a bar graph or pie chart of the results.

Math
1. Teach students how to accurately estimate the answers to calculations. Give them a work sheet and time how long it takes them to complete it. After they have completed their estimations, follow up

the exercise by timing them while they calculate the answers. Give them scores that show the difference in the time it takes to estimate versus work the problems.

2. Ask each student to estimate how many days he or she can go without watching television. Chart the actual results against their estimates. Perhaps require a parent signature to ensure accuracy.

Social Studies

1. Have students predict future events based on past patterns. ("Last January we had ten days of rainy-day schedule; How many will we have this January?" "How many lesson interruptions do we predict for today?") Have students determine how they will test their predictions.

2. Make a time capsule of future predictions (one month from now, end of the school year, five years, and so on). Put the predictions in a file and open them as they become current. (Save the five-year predictions for a future class to hear.)

3. Ask the class to predict how many Constitutional amendments or Bill of Rights the average person knows. Have students make different predictions based on the age of the people they ask. Make up a simple survey for them to check their predictions.

Physical Education

Guess who is going to win a game and then play the game to find out. Try to pick games that different kinds of students are good at.

Strategy 3

Charting and Graphing

In Brief

In lesson 1 students will learn how to use six graphic organizers and how to decipher unfamiliar graphic organizers. In lesson 2 students practice making five graphic organizers. In lesson 3 students learn how to decide what kind of graphic organizer will best represent a particular set of information.

Objective

To teach students when and how to use various graphs to represent various kinds of information

Background

Graphing is a visual way to display mathematical information. The ability to read and understand graphs increases comprehension. The ability to create appropriate graphs improves students' projects and displays and ultimately increases their comprehension of what they study.

Lesson 1: Reading Charts

Time

45 minutes (includes 10 minutes prep time)

Materials

one copy for each student of the Graphic Organizer Examples

Preparation

Make copies of the Graphic Organizer Examples for each student. Draw the graphs on the chalkboard or overhead projector.

Focus

Draw the following graph on the board, and ask students to try to explain what it means. Allow some discussion.

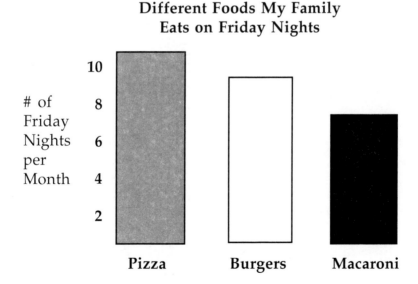

Ask students, "What is the first thing we should look at when we read a chart?" Allow brainstorming and discussion; when a student suggests the title or heading, write that up on the chalkboard and ask why that comes first. Students need to understand that the title or heading gives them the main idea or the reason for the graph.

Ask students, "What is the second thing we should look for?" Allow discussion until someone suggests the subheads, then write that on the chalkboard and ask why subheads should be looked at second. Students need to understand that the subheads tell them the specific things being measured or shown on the graph. Ask them, "What is the last thing we then look at?" Encourage discussion until students suggest the graph lines, colors, and so on, then write those on the board. Explain that the lines and colors are how students learn exactly what the graph wants to say about the main idea and the subheadings.

Draw the following graph on the board or overhead. Ask students, "What is wrong with this graph?" They should understand that, without the subheadings, they cannot know what is being compared or measured; they can only make wild guesses, which isn't a very helpful way to learn.

FAVORITE TV SHOWS

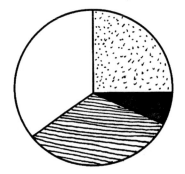

Teach

Step 1: Divide the class into groups of four or five. Give each group one of the graphs on page 216.

Step 2: Tell each group that their mission is to figure out what the graph is saying. Each group should pick an artist to draw the blank graph on the board or an overhead transparency, two illustrators to color in the graph, a writer to fill in the title and subheadings, and a reporter to explain the meaning of the graph to the rest of the class. (This process gives them practice making graphs.)

Step 3: Let each group make and discuss their graph in front of the class.

Step 4: Talk about how each graph is unique. The most important thing for students to understand is that each graph measures and compares information in a different way.

Graphic Organizer Examples

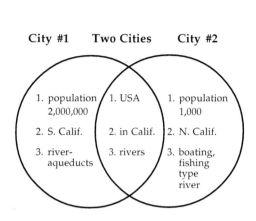

City #1   Two Cities   City #2

City #1:
1. population 2,000,000
2. S. Calif.
3. river-aqueducts

Two Cities:
1. USA
2. in Calif.
3. rivers

City #2:
1. population 1,000
2. N. Calif.
3. boating, fishing type river

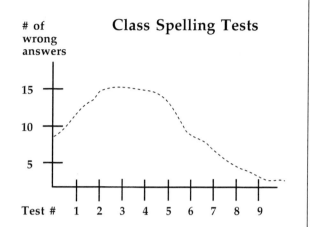

Class Spelling Tests

# of wrong answers

15
10
5

Test #   1   2   3   4   5   6   7   8   9

Students' Favorite Class at Foster Elementary

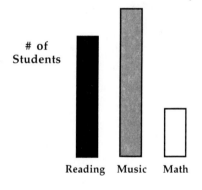

# of Students

Reading   Music   Math

What People Were Watching on TV, August 14, 7:00 PM

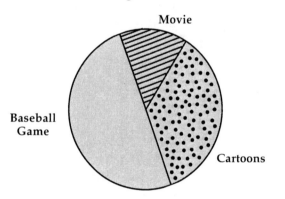

Movie

Baseball Game

Cartoons

What Jim Does After School

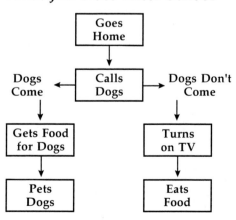

Goes Home

Calls Dogs

Dogs Come → Gets Food for Dogs → Pets Dogs

Dogs Don't Come → Turns on TV → Eats Food

Life of Arnold Biggs

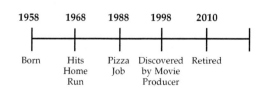

1958   1968   1988   1998   2010

Born   Hits Home Run   Pizza Job   Discovered by Movie Producer   Retired

Multliple Intelligences Made Easy © 1999 Zephyr Press, Inc., Tucson, Arizona

Step 5: Ask students to open their math, social studies, or science textbooks to find examples of graphic organizers. Ask for student volunteers to decipher the meaning of a few random samples.

Reflect

Ask the class, "Could the information in a graphic organizer be written in paragraph or report form? Which way is better? How is a graphic organizer different from a paragraph?"

Lesson 2: Making a Graph

Time

40 minutes (includes 5 minutes prep time)

Materials

one copy for each student of the Graphic Organizers work sheet

one copy for each student of information handout (page 213)

thought journals or drawing paper

Preparation

Make copies of organizers. Set up the overhead or chalkboard.

Focus

Write the following information on the chalkboard or projector while you say it to the class: "A survey of people at a grocery store showed that four liked to drink soda at dinner, ten liked to drink water, and two liked to drink milk." Ask students, "How can we show that information in a bar graph?" Ask for a student volunteer to draw the graph on the board. Keep asking for volunteers to add things until all the needed elements (title, subheadings, graphics, and number labels) are in place.

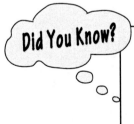

Did You Know?

Here's a wild statistic for students to graph! The average human brain is only 2 percent of a human's body weight, but the human brain uses 25 percent of the oxygen acquired by the body (Louis 1983, 26).

Name: _____

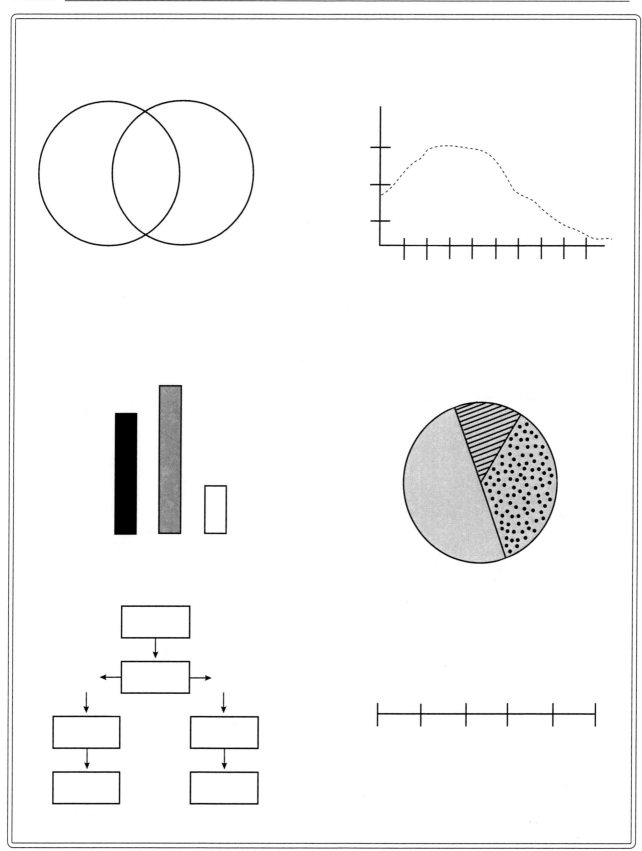

Teach

Step 1: Divide the class into groups of four or five and give each group a page of blank graphs and a page of information.

Step 2: Tell students they are to read the information and then choose a graphic organizer. Suggest that they pick the organizer to use, then draw their own in the group. They will graph the information in the graph they have chosen.

Step 3: Let each group share its finished graph and explain the information to the class.

Reflect

Ask students, "Which is easier, reading a graph or making a graph from written information? Why?"

Lesson 3: Choosing the Best Kind of Graph

Time

40 minutes (includes 5 minutes prep time)

Materials

one copy for each student of Graphic Organizers work sheet

one copy for each student of information handout

Preparation

Make copies of organizers and information.

Focus

Ask students to pick a graphic organizer and make a graph to go with the following information: "Mr. Vegas comes home to take care of his animals. If the animals are playing and don't see him, he stops and has lunch before getting them their food. If the animals see him right away and stop playing, he feeds the animals first, then eats his own lunch. After he and the animals eat, he goes outside to water the grass." Let various volunteers graph the information. It should end up looking like the chart on page 214.

Teach

Divide the class into six groups. Give each group a copy of the graphs and the information paragraphs. Ask students to work together to match their paragraph to the graph that should be used. As a class, guide each group to choose the correct organizer: paragraph 1 = bar graph or pie chart; paragraph 2 = time line; paragraph 3 = Venn diagram; paragraph 4 = flow chart; paragraph 5 = line graph; and paragraph 6 = bar graph.

1

One group of friends lives on the east side of town. They like to get together and have pizza on Friday nights. They spend their time at one person's house, play cards, and order food for delivery. A second group of friends likes to meet on Wednesdays at the local pizzeria. They all come from different parts of town and like to meet to play cards. Bill belongs to both groups of friends.

2

Jill went to the same school for five years. She started in the first grade and left for middle school in the sixth grade. In first grade she could not spell and had trouble with tests. Her average test score was 50 percent. In second grade her scores went up to 60 percent. In third grade her scores went up to 80 percent. In both the fourth and fifth grades she averaged 90 percent on her tests.

3

Mary played on three different sports teams. Her favorite sport was softball and there were ten people on her team. She was a great soccer player and there were twelve people on her soccer team. Basketball was not her favorite but she still played on a team of six people.

4

At the big end-of-the-year party there were one hundred people. Fifty people stayed until the party ended at 11 p.m. Twenty people stayed until 10 p.m., and thirty other people stayed until 8 p.m.

5

When Mike comes home from work he takes off his shoes and gets out the *TV Guide* to look for a show he likes. If one of his favorite shows is on, he turns on the television and watches for about an hour. If none of his favorites is on, he puts up his feet and takes a nap instead.

6

At 8 a.m. Sara wakes to go to school. Her school begins at 9 a.m. Her class stops for lunch at noon and they go out for afternoon recess at 2 p.m. Sara comes home from school at 3 p.m., eats a snack, then plays until dinner at 6 p.m.

Reflect

Discuss the answers to the questions: "How do you decide which graphic organizer to use? Why does it matter?"

Follow-up and Extension

Have students design graphic organizers to chart familiar things such as the month's lunch menus, number of rainy days versus overcast days versus sunny days, a time line of the year's history units (Sept. = American Indian, Oct. = Explorers, and so on), TV programs watched the night before.

Applying the Strategy to Curriculum

Science

1. Use flow charts to map the steps in a scientific experiment.
2. Use pie charts to show how much of Earth's surface is water, or to show how much of the human body is water.
3. Use time lines to show the sequence of scientific discoveries and inventions throughout history.
4. Use Venn diagrams to compare two animal species.

Mr. Vegas and His Animals

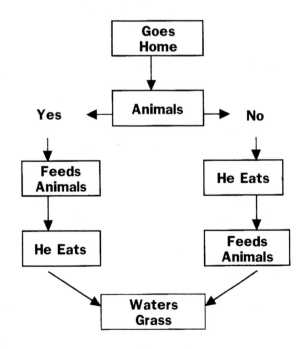

1   Carmen runs a business that sells three things: neckties, shirts, and pants. Sixty percent of her profits come from selling pants. The rest of her profits come equally from the neckties and the shirts.

2   In 1985, Jim Brown graduated from college. In 1988, he was hired by a newspaper to write an editorial column. By 1990 he was writing for twenty well-known publications, and in 1995, the *New York Times* hired him as an editor.

3   Sasha hates to go to the movies. Her favorite thing to do at night is to take walks with her mom. Mary loves to go to the movies, but she also likes to take walks with Sasha and her mom. Both girls like to read and play basketball, but Sasha only reads on weekends while Mary reads every day. Sasha is a great cook, but Mary prefers to spend her time carving wood.

4   Jos first turns on his computer, then he logs onto the Internet. If he has no e-mail messages, he writes a few notes to friends. If he finds messages in his computer mailbox, he answers those before writing notes to his friends.

5   Joe played soccer for six years. In his first year he scored ten goals. In his second and third year he could not make it to every practice and he scored only three goals each year. In his fourth year he was on a team with his best friend and he loved it, and he scored fourteen goals. In the last two years, Joe's friend had moved and he wasn't playing as hard; he scored five goals each year.

6   Thirty people were interviewed to see what school subject they liked best: fifteen said they liked social studies the best, ten said science, and only five said they liked spelling the best.

Language Arts

1. Use Venn diagrams to compare plots, characters, or settings.
2. Use flow charts to show a character's decision-making process.
3. Use time lines to plot the events of a story.
4. Use line graphs to chart the moods (good mood = high on the graph, bad = low) of a character through each chapter.

Social Studies

1. Use Venn diagrams to compare cultures, people in history, ideas and beliefs, and so on.
2. Use time lines to chart historical events, to show causes and effects, or to clarify a chain of events.
3. Use line graphs to chart the economic successes (using mean income, average wage, or number of unemployed people) or population changes in a town or state.
4. Use bar graphs or pie charts to plot the choices or opinions of people in history (for example, 40 percent of U.S. citizens were against slavery, 20 percent were for slavery, 30 percent were undecided).

Physical Education

1. Use Venn diagrams to compare the rules of two different sports.
2. Use time lines to show the changes in a sport over time.
3. Use bar graphs to show the favorite sports teams of class members.

9

Naturalist Intelligence

Naturalist intelligence involves the skills of observation of, classification within, and interaction with nature. Animal specialists, herbalists, biologists, nature artists, botanists, and even molecular biologists use naturalist skills and intelligence to observe and classify, organize and find patterns that reveal links among and separations between species. The intelligence reveals itself in childhood; children with strong naturalist intelligences love to sit and watch nature and animals; collect things and organize their collections; and name and sort any objects, even objects outside of nature, such as designer shoes and cars. When students show particular abilities to note fine details and differences, even between commercial products such as clothing or snack foods, they are to some degree using the naturalist intelligence.

The strategies in this chapter encourage children to foster this intelligence by collecting things, organizing those collections, observing and interacting with nature by looking for patterns, similarities, and differences. Encourage this type of interaction and find ways to incorporate these skills into the classroom experience.

Strategy 1

Collection Connection

In Brief

Students gather collections and create displays, then organize and label their collections.

Objectives

To spark student interest in creating a collection

To encourage students to see the slight differences that can lead to sorting and categorizing their collections

Background

Some students may already have collections of shells, stones, or even candy containers at home. Others may never have considered the prospect of collecting objects with something in common. By encouraging this practice through school lessons, you may spark an interest that has not yet been fostered and may encourage those that have embarked on collections to refine and organize their thinking.

Lesson 1: Class Leaf Collection

Time

Part 1: 30 minutes for leaf drawing and preparation

Part 2: 30 minutes one week later for making display

Did You Know?

When Jane Goodall was a young girl, her naturalist tendencies were already very evident to her family. She disappeared one day, and the whole family began a frantic search of their farm and neighboring farms without success. She appeared hours later, covered in hay and looking exhilarated. She had been hiding in the chicken coop for the entire day because she wanted to see firsthand the entire process of an egg being laid.

Materials

index cards

pencils

drawing paper

thick books

napkins or paper towels

Preparation

Ask students to bring in three different leaves from bushes or trees around their homes, neighborhoods, or parks. The leaves can be any kind; if you begin this lesson in the fall, remind them that some leaves will have fallen from the trees and it is okay to collect those. Tell them to note where and when they find each leaf so that they can use that information later.

Focus

Ask students if they have ever noticed the wide variety of leaves in the world. What are some of the differences they have noticed?

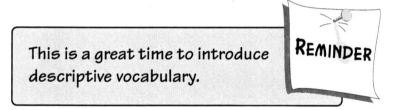

This is a great time to introduce descriptive vocabulary.

REMINDER

Teach Part 1

Step 1: Ask students to draw their three leaves as carefully as possible. They should pretend their pencil tips are small ants or bugs slowly crawling around the edge of the leaf. They will use pencil or pen to draw in any lines or veins and to show the outline and the stem shapes. These drawings offer students opportunities to take very close notice of their leaves; students can use them in their display and labeling activities as if they were photographs.

Step 2: Ask students to place their leaves between two napkins or paper towels, then to place the leaves in thick books, and close them to flatten the leaves to render them easy to display. Students can use the drawings and the leaves to label, sort, and organize in later lessons.

Teach Part 2

Step 1: One week later, students take out their flattened leaves. They glue the leaves onto thick paper, cardboard, or index cards. Students can list the following information under each leaf and each drawing, if you choose:

▶ date and season found

▶ location found

▶ color of leaf when found

▶ size (length and width; this is a great opportunity for them to practice metric measurement)

▶ noticeable features (thick visible or hidden veins; difference between top and underneath; waxy skin; smooth or jagged edges; this is a great opportunity to introduce descriptive vocabulary)

You may want to display the leaf collections or drawings in a book or on a bulletin board.

Reflect

Ask students if they notice anything about leaves that they had not noticed before. Discuss how collecting and preparing leaves for display makes us pay closer attention to the details.

Follow-up and Extension

Encourage students to pick up more leaves for the class collection when they are out on day trips or vacations with their families. Use the class leaf collection to do the sorting and grouping activities in strategy 2. You might also ask them to collect stones and pebbles.

Lesson 2: Gathering Gold Mine

Time

45 to 60 minutes

Materials

one bag for each student

thought journals

Preparation

You may need to ask permission to tour the grounds of the school or neighborhood. You may want parent volunteers to help keep an eye on students as they wander.

Start a class time when students bring in their collections. Ask them to talk about their favorite items, their method of labeling or organizing, and the interests that made them begin the collection.

REMINDER

Focus

Ask students if any of them have anything they collect. Perhaps they have a favorite animal character and they have acquired key chains, stuffed animals, and stickers featuring that character. Perhaps they have a box of seashells or stones at home. Let students that have begun such collections share them with the class. Ask them how they got started. What made them want to collect those items?

Teach

Step 1: Announce to students that they are all going to have an opportunity to create their own collections of items they find in nature. Invite them to discuss what people can find on the ground simply by walking around outside. Ask if any students have spent time looking on the ground as they walk to school. What did they see there? Some students will mention trash and litter. Trash and litter can make a very interesting collection.

Step 2: Go over any class rules for behavior outside: no crossing streets, staying within your view, and so on. Discuss items that, in the interest of safety, students should not pick up: needles, sharp objects, items in deep holes or crevasses. Give bags to students.

Step 3: Spend 30 minutes wandering the school grounds or the local neighborhood. Allow students to collect a variety of things, but encourage them to consider which kind of thing they would most like to collect and look at.

Step 4: Return to the room and allow students to spread their collections on their desktops. They will discuss their finds with their classmates. Ask them to choose which items they will keep and which they will discard. They label their "keepers" by putting them in one bag with a name, the date on which they were found, and the location at which they were found marked on the outside.

Reflect

Ask students to share their thoughts and feelings about the experience of looking for things to collect. What did they like? Not like? Did anyone find many types of one thing, such as different bottle tops, for instance? Discuss what a person might choose to do with a collection. Ask them to put their thoughts into their journals.

Follow-up and Extension

Organize the collected items in strategy 2. Students continue to add to their collections by looking around at home and when they are on day trips.

Lesson 3: Displays and Scrapbooks

Time

depends on size of collections; might need 45 minutes for larger collections or more than 8 items

Materials

construction paper

shoebox tops or cardboard sheets

index cards

tape

glue

if school has book or scrapbook making material a scrapbook can work for a class or individual collection

students' or teacher's collections (rocks, shells, leaves, trash)

Preparation

If you have access to any organized collections such as stamps, scrapbooks, bugs, display them for students.

Focus

Ask students how they might display a collection attractively so that it evokes others' interest. Discuss color combinations, labeling, size of items, and so on. If you have examples, look over those together and discuss what makes their arrangements attractive.

Teach

Step 1: Let individual students work alone on their own collections or together if they believe they can combine their collections successfully with another student's. Decide how to display the collections (index cards work best for me). Or you might ask your students to spend some time deciding how to display their collections in interesting manners. They can glue objects to cardboard or tape them to paper and create a scrapbook. They might have a file of index cards with different items or a poster board. They can use Styrofoam or cardboard and attach items with pushpins or tacks. Pressed flowers and plants look nice in a book or on a bulletin display. Note: A parent or other helper with a glue gun can help make the creation of displays particularly easy.

Step 2: Once they have made the decision regarding how to display their collections, students create labels for each item. The label should contain the following basic information:

> ▶ description, including measurements when possible
> ▶ location where item was found
> ▶ date item was found
> ▶ comments or special observations regarding item

Encourage students to label items they collect immediately for the sake of their memories.

Applying the Strategy to the Curriculum

Science

1. Students collect pictures of various animal and plant species and label the pictures with such information as where the animal lives, how big it grows, its diet.

Language Arts

1. Students write about their collections. Possible writing prompts include

   Three things that would really make my collection special

   The steps to creating a great collection

   The collection that buried the kid in room eleven.

2. Students use attributes of the collection to develop a list of wonderful adjectives. They use the list to write a poem about the collections. The poem structure might work like this:

   My collection is . . .

   scruffy, layered, and old

   smooth, shiny, and wide,

   rough, cracked, and peeling,

   stones.

Math

1. Students create a class line graph that shows the number of items added to the collections over a week or a month.

Social Studies

1. Students create and collect imitation "baseball cards" by drawing explorers, key persons in American history, and so on, on the front of an index card, then listing data such as birth date, death date, what they are famous for, places lived, on the other side of the card or under the picture.

Strategy 2

Honing Your Hierarchy

In Brief

Students practice organizing and sorting materials to decide how to organize their own collections.

Objectives

To help students see the similarities and differences between their collection items

To help students see shape, color, and size relationships among items

Background

One key characteristic of people utilizing the naturalist intelligence is that they are successful at sorting animals and items based on shared characteristics.

Lesson 1: Typecasting

Time

30 to 40 minutes, but can be longer depending on the size of collections

Materials

previously collected and labeled collections
items to create displays

Preparation

Once the class or student collections from strategy 1 are on cards or displays and labeled, students can begin sorting and grouping.

Focus

Ask students who are wearing blue to stand. Then ask students to strike a pose if they are wearing blue and red. Then ask anyone in that group who is also wearing white to strike a pose with their hands on their heads. Explain to the class that you have just sorted them into groups based on characteristics of color. Ask them to tell you what is true about all of the children who are standing. Next ask them to tell you what is true about the group of children who are standing but also striking a pose. Ask them finally to tell you about the group who is standing and striking a pose with their hands on their heads. Finally, ask them to describe the children who are not standing.

Teach

Step 1: Discuss different sorting possibilities as a class. Then discuss the criteria students would use to separate their own collections into two groups. By shape? Color? Size?

Step 2: Discuss sorting the class or individual collections into three groups. What new criteria would students use? Does every group in a collection need to be exactly the same size or can the number of items in the groups vary?

Step 3: As a class for the class collection or as individuals, students determine how they might divide collections into five or six groups. To sort into five or six groups, children will be looking at more than one feature: size and shape, color and special characteristics, and so on. They write the features on index cards, label the group, and describe it briefly (for example: group 1: jagged edges, green leaves, larger than 4 inches). They lay the index cards with the appropriate groups. Some students may find that they end up with one or two items that do not fit into any of the categories they arranged. Discuss individually if the item looks like it belongs with a particular group or whether it should be its own group.

Follow-up and Extension

Once students are happy with the way they have organized their collections, they might use cardboard, foam, scrapbooks, or boxes to display their sorted collections with titles to delineate groupings.

Lesson 2: The Ladder of Importance

Time

This lesson will need to be taught again and again for practice. It can be as short as a class thinking activity that takes 15 minutes.

Materials

board or big paper for brainstorming

Preparation

You might want to prepare a list of topics that students can easily break into subtopics.

Focus

Ask students, "How many different kinds of animals can you name?" Create a class list of all kinds.

Teach

Step 1: Explain to students that they can create categories for anything. Creating a category means to recognize that items can be grouped together in ways that make sense.

Step 2: Ask if the list of animals can be broken down into two types somehow. Let them throw out ideas and discuss whether all the animals would fit into one group or the other, for example, wild and domestic, furred and no fur, larger than humans and smaller than humans. Once you have two subtopics, write them as headings on the board and list the animals under the appropriate headings (see example).

Wild	Domestic
lion	cow
elephant	dog
alligator	cat
lizard	chicken
eagle	parrot
owl	horse
worm	goldfish
ant	

Step 3: Students look at one list at a time and divide that list into two or three more subgroups. For instance, wild animals could have subgroups: animals with fur, animals with feathers, animals with neither fur nor feathers.

Step 4: Practice again with sports. Ask students if you were going to create a group called "sports," what they would put into that grouping. Let them list items that fall under sports: baseball, basketball, golf, gymnastics, fields, equipment, bats, balls.

Step 5: Ask students if they can see subgroups that could be made under the big group. Which items on the list go together in a smaller group? Encourage them to discover that you can create a subgroup under sports called "equipment" that might have balls, bats, clubs, and such in it. You could also create another subgroup called "ballgames" that could contain baseball, basketball, football, and soccer. Make enough groups that everything you have listed is included in a group.

Reflect

Ask students if any of the items fit into more than one group. Can they add items you did not have before into any of the subgroups you have listed under sports? Look back to the animal lists. Do any animals fit into more than one group? Are there animals they can add to any subgroups that were not listed before?

Follow-up and Extension

Divide the class into groups and give each group a big topic, such as school, buildings, news, pets, toys, games, hobbies, activities, shoes. Let each group list the things that fall under that topic. Then invite them to determine how to break their lists into subgroups of the big topic. The groups share their organizational ideas with the rest of the class.

Lesson 3: Twenty Questions

Time

15 to 20 minutes the first time you play the game; you can easily play in 10 minutes as a filler

Materials

chalkboard

chalk for scorekeeping

Focus

Ask students if they would enjoy learning a thinking game.

Teach

Step 1: Remind students about sorting collections into different groups. Remind them how you could have a larger group, such as all the people standing that were wearing blue, and within that larger group, a smaller group, such as people who were wearing blue and also red. The same thing is true for all people, animals, places, and things in the world.

Step 2: Tell them the game they are going to play involves guessing the correct person, place, animal, or thing in twenty questions or fewer. Each question must be answerable with "yes" or "no." Tell them you are going to try it one time to show them what it is like.

Step 3: Choose something like leopard. Say, "I am thinking of a person, place, animal, or thing, and you have twenty questions to guess it." One student tallies the questions on the chalkboard. Let students ask questions. As they ask, coach them to reword questions so that they can be answered with a yes or a no. Do not answer questions with any other responses. If they are able to guess in fewer than twenty questions, congratulate them on winning the game. If not, congratulate them on a nice try, then offer to give them some big hints on how to make the game work best.

For example, suppose you chose leopard. You would say, "I am thinking of a person, place, or thing. Can you guess what it is in fewer than twenty questions?" Students begin by asking, "Is it a dog or a cat?" Respond, "Can you reword your question so I can answer with either a yes or no?" Students reword: "Is it a cat?" "Yes." After the first game, here are some hints you can give students:

HINT 1 Listen carefully to what other children ask so you will not repeat questions that have already been answered. Explain that if one child asks if the thing you are thinking is a mammal and you answer yes, then another child asks if it is an animal, the second student has wasted a question.

HINT 2 Because you could be thinking about *anything* in the world, it is important that they narrow categories before making exact guesses. You could be thinking of a table in this room or an animal in Africa or a planet in outer space. Think of some general yes or no questions that would help to quickly narrow the possibilities. Help students arrive at such questions as, "Is it a living thing?" "Is it smaller than this room?" "Can you find it in this country?"

After you have discussed the possibilities, try twenty questions again. Some students will take the hints well and others will take longer to learn the techniques, but over time the game will teach them to narrow the possibilities and to naturally sort and organize information from general to specific.

Reflect

Ask students what happens when they start the game with very specific questions, such as, "Is it a chair?" Students should respond or understand that it will likely take more than twenty tries to guess the item.

Follow-up and Extension

Students draw a flow chart of questions: Is it on our planet? Is it a living thing? Is it a mammal? Does it have four legs? Do people have them as pets? Can you find it in Africa? Is it a member of the feline family? Is it a lion? Is it a leopard?

Work backward to create the flow chart. Say the creature is a leopard; what will be the last yes or no question? The one before that? The one before that?

Applying the Strategy to the Curriculum

Science

1. Use collections to launch a study of animal and plant kingdoms. Classifying objects leads nicely into classifying living creatures. Look at the way scientists have classified living things. Discuss why they group different animals together under categories such as felines; what is it that these groups have in common?

2. Occasionally, post a picture of part of an animal or plant, such as a lobster claw. Ask students these questions: What animal or plant has this part? What do you think the animal uses this part for? Draw the part.

Math

1. Students create bar graphs of their sorted collections. How many of each type do they have?

2. Students draw each collected item on individual index cards, then organize the cards into rows and columns that make sense.

Language Arts

1. Students read about stamp collecting in an encyclopedia, a news or magazine article, or on the Internet. Discuss how collectors organize their stamps and why.

Post a flow chart that shows general questions that evolve into more specific ones for the students to emulate.

REMINDER

2. Practice coming up with a main idea and details to support it in writing paragraphs. First, students write main idea topics such as "wild animals," then they write three detail topics, such as "lions, tigers, bears." They write a sentence for the main idea and one for each subtopic.

Social Studies

1. Students practice organizing learning. Give them main ideas such as colonies or American Indian tribes. Students list subgroups, such as northern, middle, and southern colonies; and Southwest, Northwest, and Eastern Woodland tribes. They list specific details under the subgroups.

Strategy 3

Connecting to Nature

In Brief

This strategy involves enlivening the senses through close observation and interaction with nature.

Objectives

To help children better connect with the world around them

To heighten children's awareness and appreciation for nature and the unique qualities of the human senses

Background

Often, children are separated from nature and the sensitivities that being in nature can invoke in an individual, especially if the children live in suburban or urban areas.

Lesson 1: Observation Station

Time

varied and individual; depends on whether you set this activity up as a center or as full class lesson

Materials

magnifiers (at least one per every two children)

class set of varying stones or rocks (at least one per every two children) pencils

paper

Preparation
Pass out magnifiers and stones.

Focus
Ask students how many of them have ever spent some time looking closely, very closely, at an object. What have they looked at? Why were they looking so closely? What did they notice?

Teach

Step 1: Show students the set of rocks from the front of the classroom. Ask them to draw the rocks as they see them from that distance.

Step 2: Drop each stone from your waist height to the desktop and ask students to listen to whether the stones make different sounds. Then ask them if they think the rocks feel or smell different from one another. Let them discuss and state their opinions. Some will complain that you can't really tell from that distance. Explain that they will have an opportunity to touch, smell, hear, and look at the stones more closely; that you would like to hear about their discoveries. Tell them successful scientists have excellent observation abilities; they can really discern very slight differences. Explain that the magnifier will also help them to look even more closely than their eyes will allow.

Step 3: Students write headings *sight, sound, touch,* and *smell* on their papers; encourage them to write or draw what they notice about their stone under each heading. Pass out the stones and magnifiers.

Step 4: When students have spent some time looking at just one stone, ask them to share any surprising details they noticed with the rest of the class. Some might say they noticed little specks of color under the magnifier that their eyes didn't see. Some might say the stone made a high sound when they dropped it on the table.

Step 5: Discuss their various observations, then ask them to trade, observe their new stones closely, and write their observations down. Ask if they noticed differences between the two stones. What kinds of differences did they notice? If time permits, let them look at three or more stones. You will find some students look very quickly and are finished and other students have a more honed attention to detail. The more you encourage them to take their time and look closely and the more you ask them to share their discoveries, the more students will attempt to look closely for specific details.

Reflect

List some of the differences students noticed on the board.

Follow-up and Extension

Set up a center in which students can look at dead bugs, shells, plants, material, or science specimens. Make sure the center has a magnifier, pencils, and paper for drawing and taking notes. A place for students to post their observations would be appealing and useful.

Lesson 2: Turning up Sensory Volumes

Time

If you do each sense separately, the lessons can take about 10 minutes each; if you study them all at once, I would allow at least 35 minutes.

Materials

board for taking notes on class discussion

spices (cinnamon, onion, oregano, basil, rosemary, and so on)

Preparation

Divide spices into small cups for easy handling.

Focus

Ask students to name their senses and to explain why they think they have senses.

Teach

Step 1: If at all possible, take students outside. Something about the sounds and smells in the outdoors makes the senses come alive.

Step 2: Ask students to sit in a circle and tell them you are going to practice turning the volume up on their senses. By becoming more attuned to sights, sounds, feelings, and smells, they will be better able to observe closely. Explain to them that scientists in particular rely very much on being very attuned to their senses to be able to observe closely.

Step 3: Hearing—Ask students to close their eyes. The sense of sight is something we rely on so much that it will be easier for them to focus on other senses if their eyes are closed. Ask them to listen very closely for a few seconds, then share some of the things they heard. Next, they close their eyes and listen for only sounds that are within a few feet of where they are sitting. Ask what they were able to hear. Ask them to close their eyes again and gradually try to hear sounds farther and farther away. After a few moments, they share all the sounds they could hear at a distance. Ask them what surprised them about the experience.

Step 4: Sight—Try the activity with sight. Students look very closely at what they can notice within a few feet of where they are seated. Then they look farther away. They do it one more time, looking as far into the distance as they can see.

Step 5: Smell—Students do the same progression with smells. Bring out the spices. Students turn up their senses of smell and identify the various spices.

Step 6: Touch—Ask them to turn up the volume on feeling. They notice the feelings when their bodies press against the ground, then notice the feeling of clothes on their skin. Finally, they notice more subtle feelings, such as the wind or cool air and so on.

Step 7: Taste—Ask students to do this step at home. Blindfolded or with eyes closed, they identify a variety of tastes that someone picks out for them

Did You Know?

What appear to be silly ideas often turn out the best. I gave a science observation project to my fifth graders. They were to observe closely a living organism for one week and to take notes on their observations, including what the animal ate and drank, how it moved, and so on. One child announced that she intended to watch her ficus plant, and the class roared with laughter. But when her notes came back, they were by far the most detailed and interesting in the class. She had noted the weight of the potted plant before and after watering it, then again later in the day. She had noted ways the leaves bent to expose themselves to sunlight, and each new sprout and bud at the end of particular stems. She had even noted the interaction between the plant and insects that had landed on the leaves. Her classmates and I were duly impressed by her powers of observation.

Reflect

Ask students what happens when they turn up the volume on their senses. List their thoughts on the board.

Follow-up and Extension

Bring in various items with scents and ask students to identify the smells. Look at works of art or listen to music and ask them to turn up the volume on those senses and tell you what they notice.

Lesson 3: Bring the Bugs In

Time

varied and intermittent

Materials

bug jars or bug boxes

water

bowls

magnifiers

large butcher paper or journal sheets

Preparation

Let students and their families know you have an interest in inviting bugs and animals to visit the classroom. Find out if any students have unusual pets to share (lizards, birds, mice, ant farms). Invite bug-interested students to bring in insects they catch for the classroom to view and study. Snails also work great.

Focus

Whenever animal visitors come to your classroom, introduce them to students. Explain that the visitor gives the whole class an opportunity to learn more about that particular species.

Teach

Step 1: Ask students what they already know or think they know about the kind of animal. List what they already know. Ask them to name some animal relatives, body parts, food, and so on. Ask them to list this prior knowledge on butcher paper or journal sheets.

Step 2: Measure the visitor, if possible. Ask students to draw the creature as a class. Label body parts. Give students magnifiers to get close-up views of the animal.

Step 3:   Create a class record sheet that names the creature, gives its measurements, and all the facts they already knew about the animal. Then leave space for observations of the animal.

Step 4:   Over the day or days you have the visitor, remind students to stop periodically to check on its behavior. Write observations on your class record sheet.

Step 5:   Based on classroom observations, ask students what its body parts do, what it eats, what other creatures it may be related to.

Step 6:   Ask students to research the animal on the Internet or in an encyclopedia. They will find whether any of their guesses are correct; discuss any new findings, adding them to your class record.

Step 7:   Release the visitor into the wild or back to its owner. Students keep class journal pages to add to when you have your next visitor.

Reflect

Ask students why it was useful to observe and make guesses about the visitor before looking up information in sources. Explain that they might have discovered something new about the creature, just as biologists do when they observe and research animals. Guessing often sparks interest and ideas better than just reading information in a book.

Follow-up and Extension

Ask other visitors to come into class, for example, local naturalists might bring in exotic or interesting animals for a visit. Do long-term studies in which students see animals go through entire cycles, such as butterflies growing in a cocoon or silkworms.

Applying the Strategy to the Curriculum

Science

1.   Research bug and animal visitors and write science reports about each species.

2.   Interview scientists to find out how they use their senses to help them in their scientific inquiries.

Math

1.   Use metric measurements to find the sizes of various animal visitors and, when possible, their parts. Create a chart that compares sizes of the various animals.

Language Arts

1. Ask students to write stories and plays about the animal visitors. The stories and plays might reveal important behaviors and facts about the creatures. Learn as a class what *anthropomorphic* means. Learn the root, the prefixes and suffixes. List examples of anthropomorphic stories students have read (*Charlotte's Web, Stuart Little,* etc.)

Social Studies

1. As a class, students make a world map of animal species. They cut out or draw pictures of animals and tack, glue, or staple them onto a world map in the countries of their natural habitats.

2. Students discover how animals and plants are used differently in different cultures.

Compare and Contrast

In Brief

By drawing connections and making comparisons students learn how to communicate the similarities and differences between two things.

Objectives

To help students compare and contrast various items

To draw connections among different items

Background

Naturalist intelligence is tied to the ability to discern similarities and differences between things. Discerning even the slightest differences and being able to communicate those differences allows the naturalist to determine the evolution of various species. This essential skill is part of the art of classification and key to the naturalist intelligence.

Lesson 1: Drawing Connections

Time

25 minutes

Materials

pictures of a variety of animals

photocopies or an overhead of drawings of paws (see figure 1 below)

paper

pencils

Preparation

Write this sentence on the board: A footprint of a squirrel is like the footprint of a _____ except

Focus

Ask students if they notice that animals, even animals that are the same species, do not always look alike. What are some differences they have noticed in cats? (color, length of fur, size)

Teach

Step 1: Tell students to look at the photocopies of drawings of animal tracks (see figure 1). Ask them if they see any differences in the prints. Discuss each slight difference they can see. Ask them to guess the reasons for the differences. Create a Venn diagram that lists similarities and differences. Discuss students' findings and ask them to fill in the blanks in the sentences.

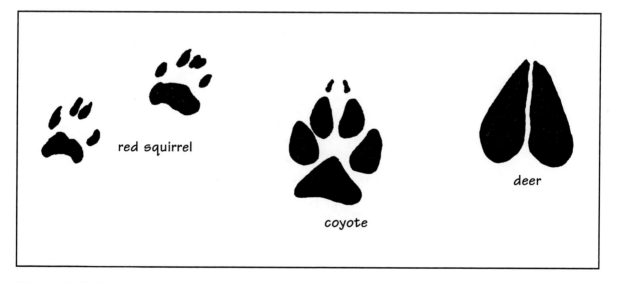

Figure 1. Animal tracks

Reflect

Ask students to imagine the types of feet that created the paw prints. Have them draw and describe the feet of the animals. Ask if they can think of any reasons why the footprints and feet are different. Some may just discuss that the size of the animal changes the size of the print; others may explore further to discuss whether the animals walk and climb, the size needed to support the frame, and so on.

Follow-up and Extension

Students collect pictures of animals and compare their body parts to the others' body parts. Beaks make for interesting discussion, as do fish fins or eyes. Tell them to note the bottoms of the feet on their pets at home. Compare additional paw prints from a variety of animals.

Lesson 2: Leaves and Leaves

Time

25 minutes

Materials

class set of leaf drawings or overhead with drawings on it

paper for Venn diagrams

pencils

Preparation

Make an overhead or redraw the leaves on the board. As an extra help, you might collect posters and pictures of trees and leaves.

Focus

Show the picture to the class. Ask students to label the items according to where they are found in nature; do any of them remember a specific time when they noticed a leaf that looked like any of these leaves?

Teach

Step 1: Draw a three-circle Venn diagram, and ask students to list in the middle all the things that they notice are similar about the three leaves (see figure 2).

Step 2: They independently list traits unique to each leaf in the appropriate parts of the circles.

Step 3: They list the traits that two of the leaves have in common, but not the third, in the appropriate parts of the circle.

Step 4: Discuss why the leaves might have such different qualities (location, weather, size of tree).

Figure 2. Venn diagram with leaves

Reflect

Ask students which type of leaf they think they see most often in their neighborhoods. Ask them to check the leaves in their yards and on their streets, and to report their findings to the class.

Follow-up and Extension

Get out some plant or gardening books on tree types and discuss what the botanists have to say about the different types of leaves found on trees. Discuss whether needles behave differently in the fall than do flat green leaves.

Applying the Strategy to the Curriculum

Science

1. Students look at list of a particular family of animal and explain what all the different types have in common. Then they make notes regarding the differences between the members of the specific animal family. For instance, look at fish together and determine the traits present in all fish. Then try to see the differences between different types of fish.

Math

1. Students explain what is similar and different about geometric shapes. A rectangle is like a triangle except . . . A cylinder is like a cone except . . . A sphere is like a circle except . . .

Language Arts

1. Students create pictures of various paw prints that overlap. They write a story about when and how the different animals crossed one another's paths.

2. Students devise analogies that require comparisons of characteristics, such as:

   Dog is to muzzle as bird is to

   Feathers are to birds as _____ *is to mammals.*

   Claw is to bear as _____ *is to human.*

   Vein is to leaf as _____ *is to human.*

3. Define such words as *coniferous, deciduous, perennial,* and *adaptation.*

Social Studies

1. Students compare and contrast events in history, landforms in geography, or lifestyles of historic groups such as European peoples.

Bibliography

Adams, James. 1974. *Conceptual Blockbusting.* Stanford, Conn.: Stanford Alumni Association.

Armstrong, Thomas. 1987. *In Their Own Way: Discovering and Encouraging Your Child's Personal Learning Style.* New York: G. P. Putnam.

Arnold, Ellen. 1999. *The MI Strategy Bank.* Tucson, Ariz.: Zephyr Press.

Barkman, Robert. 1999. *Science through Multiple Intelligences: Patterns That Inspire Inquiry.* Tucson, Ariz.: Zephyr Press.

Benzwie, Teresa. 1987. *A Moving Experience: Dance for Lovers of Children and the Child Within.* Tucson, Ariz.: Zephyr Press.

———. 1995. *More Moving Experiences: Connecting Arts, Feelings, and Imagination.* Tucson, Ariz.: Zephyr Press.

Bowen, Jean, Carol King, and Marianne Hawkins. *Square Pegs: Building Success in School and Life through MI.* Tucson, Ariz.: Zephyr Press.

Bruetsch, Anne. 1998. *Multiple Intelligences Lesson Plan Book.* Tucson, Ariz.: Zephyr Press.

Buzan, Tony. 1977. *Make the Most of Your Mind.* New York: Simon and Schuster.

Caine, Geoffrey, Renate N. Caine, and Sam Cromwell. 1994. *MindShifts: A Brain-Based Process for Restructuring Schools and Educational Renewal.* Tucson, Ariz.: Zephyr Press.

De Bono, Edward. 1995. *Mind Power: Discover the Secrets of Creative Thinking.* New York: Dorling Kindersley.

Diamond, Marian C. 1988. *Enriching Heredity: The Impact of the Environment on the Anatomy of the Brain.* New York: Free Press.

Ellison, Launa. 1995. *The Brain: A User's Guide.* Tucson, Ariz.: Zephyr Press.

Fogarty, Robin. 1994. *How to Teach for Metacognitive Reflection.* Palatine, Ill.: Skylight.

Gardner, Howard. 1983. *Frames of Mind: The Theory of Multiple Intelligences.* New York: Basic Books.

———. 1993a. *Creating Minds.* New York: Basic Books.

———. 1993b. *Multiple Intelligences: The Theory in Practice.* New York: Basic Books.

Glock, Jenna, Maggie Meyer, and Susan Wertz. 1998. *Discovering the Naturalist Intelligence: Science in the School Yard.* Tucson, Ariz.: Zephyr Press.

Gross, Ron. 1991. *Peak Learning.* New York: G. P. Putnam.

Healy, Jane M. 1987. *Your Child's Growing Mind.* New York: Doubleday.

———. 1990. *Endangered Minds: Why Our Children Don't Think.* New York: Simon and Schuster.

Jensen, Eric P. 1988. *Super Teaching.* Del Mar, Calif.: Turning Point.

———. 1994a. "The Almost-Genius High-Energy Learning Diet." In *Turning Point Bulletin 2B.* Del Mar, Calif.: Turning Point.

———. 1994b. *The Learning Brain.* Del Mar, Calif.: Turning Point.

Klauser, Henriette Anne. 1987. *Writing on Both Sides of the Brain.* New York: Harper and Row.

Kline, Peter. 1988. *Everyday Genius.* Arlington, Va.: Great Ocean.

Kunzler, Donna. 1997. *Kid Smart* posters. Tucson, Ariz.: Zephyr Press.

Lazear, David. 1999a. *Eight Pathways of Learning: Teaching Students and Parents about Multiple Intelligences.* Tucson, Ariz.: Zephyr Press.

———. 1999b. *Eight Ways of Knowing: Teaching for Multiple Intelligences.* Palatine, Ill.: Skylight.

———. 1999c. *Eight Ways of Teaching: The Artistry of Teaching with Multiple Intelligences.* Palatine, Ill.: Skylight.

———. 1998a. *Intelligence Builders for Every Student: 44 Exercises to Expand MI in Your Classroom.* Tucson, Ariz.: Zephyr Press.

———. 1999d. *The Intelligent Curriculum: Using MI to Develop Your Students' Full Potential.* Tucson, Ariz.: Zephyr Press.

———. 1998b. *The Rubrics Way: Using MI to Assess Understanding.* Tucson, Ariz.: Zephyr Press.

Lazear, David, and Nancy Margulies. 1998. *Tap Your Multiple Intelligences* posters. Tucson, Ariz.: Zephyr Press.

Louis, David. 1983. *2001 Fascinating Facts.* New York: Ridge Press.

Margulies, Nancy. 1996. *The Magic 7: Tools for Building Your Multiple Intelligences.* Tucson, Ariz.: Zephyr Press.

———. 1991. *Mapping Inner Space.* Tucson, Ariz.: Zephyr Press.

McAuliffe, Jane, and Laura Stoskin. 1991. *What Color Is Saturday?* Tucson, Ariz.: Zephyr Press.

Ogle, Donna. 1986. "KWL: A Teaching Model That Develops Active Reading of Expository Text." *Reading Teacher* 6: 564–70.

Rose, Colin. 1985. *Accelerated Learning.* New York: Dell.

Rose, Laura. 1996. *Developing Intelligences through Literature: Ten Theme-Based Units for Growing Minds.* Tucson, Ariz.: Zephyr Press.

Udall, Anne J., and Joan E. Daniels. 1991. *Creating the Thoughtful Classroom: Strategies to Promote Student Thinking.* Tucson, Ariz.: Zephyr Press.

Webb, Terry Wyler, and Douglas Webb. 1990. *Accelerated Learning with Music.* Norcross, Ga.: Accelerated Learning Systems.

Weber, Ellen. 1995. *Roundtable Learning: Building Understanding through Enhanced MI Strategies.* Tucson, Ariz.: Zephyr Press.

Weinberger, Norman, ed. Ongoing. *Musica Newsletter.* Irvine, Calif.: Center for Neurobiology and Memory, UC Irvine.

About the Author

Bonita DeAmicis is a fifth-grade teacher in the Saugus Union School District in Santa Clarita, California. She chose to teach because it is a career that offers a lifetime of variety and room to grow. For more than ten years she has taught young children and adults in such varied subjects as general studies and gifted education, art and parenting, and in such varied environments as inner-city

schools and suburban enclaves. She uses writing as a vehicle for learning and growing as a teacher. She received her BFA from the University of Southern California. Her other book for Zephyr Press, *3 Cheers for Teaching,* leads teachers through effective strategies for making real change in their lives and work. She hopes her readers use her books as launching pads for their own growth and discovery.

Zephyr Press—Your #1 Source for Multiple Intelligences Resources

PATHWAYS OF LEARNING
Teaching Students and Parents about Multiple Intelligences
David Lazear
Foreword by Arthur Costa

Pathways of Learning is packed full of methods, tools, and techniques for teaching both students and parents about multiple intelligences. The 20 mini-lessons and more than 120 extensions include reproducible blacklines that spiral the lessons for all grade levels. There are 25 pages devoted to information for parents, and an extensive list of practical ways parents can nurture the development of the intelligences in their children.

Grades K–12+
ISBN: 1-56976-118-3
288 pages
1115-W . . . $39.95

MI STRATEGIES FOR KIDS
Featuring Brilliant Brain and Magnificent Mind
Ellen Arnold

Michelle has given up on multiplication . . . Robert's fear of bullies overshadows his love for learning . . . Lisa struggles to read . . .

Do these situations sound familiar? *MI Strategies for Kids* helps you turn your struggling students into confident learners. The series features six creatively illustrated books for your students and a teacher/parent manual that gives you an understanding of how to help *all* learners think mindfully. Lesson plans detail how to incorporate each multiple intelligences book into your existing curriculum, and "strength-based" interview strategies help you get to the heart of any learner's difficulty.

Grades K–6
ISBN: 1-56976-128-0
Set of 6 books and Teacher/Parent Manual
147-W . . . $50.00

THE MI STRATEGY BANK
Ellen Arnold

Do you often ask yourself, "How can I best teach this learner?" *The MI Strategy Bank* gives you tools to recognize how your students learn best and precise methods to instruct them more effectively. Arnold helps you define your students' strengths and shows you the way to use her multiple intelligences strategies with mini case studies of strength-based assessments. Shaded pages will help you reference each intelligence quickly and easily. You'll have strategies to improve reading, writing, spelling, math skills and more, as well as ways to prevent behavior problems when students are frustrated.

Grades K–12
ISBN: 1-56976-097-7
96 pages
1099-W . . . $19.95

MULTIPLE INTELLIGENCES LESSON PLAN BOOK
Anne Bruetsch

Look to this innovative resource for 40 reproducible Week at a Glance planners. Each week includes daily checklists for the intelligences and weekly reflection on how to apply them in your class-room. You'll get 15 additional Multiple Intelligences Lesson Plan forms that are great for unit plans, lesson plans, and activity centers. You'll also find practical suggestions for specific activities, assessments that incorporate the multiple intelligences, ways of formulating objectives to meet the cognitive, affective, and interactive needs of students, and valuable resource materials for each intelligence, including music to facilitate learning.

Grades K–12+
ISBN: 1-56976-095-0
181 pages in a 3-ring binder
1052-W . . . $30.00

3 CHEERS FOR TEACHING!
A Guide to Growing Professionally and Renewing Your Spirit
Bonita DeAmicis

An extraordinary step-by-step program that will help you uncover what you need to know in order to teach well. If you've been looking for an easy way to initiate your own professional growth plan, this simple yet transforming three-part program makes right now the perfect time to get started.

Professional Growth
ISBN: 1-56976-094-2
160 pages
1098-W . . . $29.95

TEACHING IN THE TAO
Patrick Christie

Like the *Tao Te Ching*, the ancient Chinese text, *Teaching in the Tao* provides teachers with philosophical expressions of harmony and compassion to help them in their chosen "way" of teaching. The 70 poetic reflections will inspire you to remember why you chose teaching as a profession and will help you stay in balance with daily life.

"No matter what anyone says, it's OK to be liked as a teacher. From fondness comes trust. From trust comes openness. From openness comes true learning."
—Patrick Christie

Professional Growth
ISBN: 1-56976-126-4
96 pages
1124-W . . . $11.95

BEARING WITNESS
Poetry by Teachers about Teaching
Edited by Margaret Hatcher

Margaret Hatcher has filled this magnificent volume with 120 carefully selected poems by 70 poet-teachers. With poems that run the gamut from the joy of lighting a student's inner fire to teenage suicide and celebrating the child who stands up for others to child abuse, *Bearing Witness* is packed with humanity and emotion.

Professional Growth
ISBN: 1-56976-130-2
192 pages
1149-W . . . $18.95

Order Form

Qty.	Item #	Title	Unit Price	Total

Subtotal	
Sales Tax (AZ residents, 5.6%)	
S & H (10% of subtotal–min $5.50)	
Total (U.S. funds only)	

CANADA: add 30% for S & H and G.S.T.

Name _____

Address _____

City _____

State _____ Zip _____

Phone (_____) _____

E-mail _____

Method of payment (check one):

❏ Check or Money Order ❏ Visa

❏ MasterCard ❏ Purchase Order Attached

Credit Card No. _____

Expires _____

Signature _____

☎

Please include your phone number in case we have questions about your order.

Call, write, e-mail or Fax for your FREE catalog!

Zephyr Press

P.O. Box 66006-W
Tucson, AZ 85728-6006

1-800-232-2187
520-322-5090
Fax 520-323-9402
neways2learn@zephyrpress.com

Order these resources and more any time, day or night, online at **www.zephyrpress.com** or **www.i-home-school.com**